D0700133

WITHDRAWN
UTSA LIBRARIES

The Current Crisis
in International Lending

Studies in International Economics

The Current Crisis in International Lending

Jack M. Guttentag and Richard J. Herring

THE BROOKINGS INSTITUTION
Washington, D.C.

© 1985 by
THE BROOKINGS INSTITUTION
1775 Massachusetts Avenue, N.W., Washington, D.C. 20036

Library of Congress Catalog Card Number 84-45846
ISBN 0-8157-3325-9

1 2 3 4 5 6 7 8 9

LIBRARY
**The University of Texas
At San Antonio**

Board of Trustees
Robert V. Roosa
Chairman

Andrew Heiskell
Vice Chairman;
Chairman, Executive Committee

Louis W. Cabot
Vice Chairman;
Chairman, Development Committee

Samuel H. Armacost
J. David Barnes
Vincent M. Barnett, Jr.
Barton M. Biggs
Frank T. Cary
A. W. Clausen
William T. Coleman, Jr.
Lloyd N. Cutler
Thomas Donahue
Charles W. Duncan, Jr.
Robert F. Erburu
Hanna H. Gray
Robert D. Haas
Philip M. Hawley
Amory Houghton, Jr.
Roy M. Huffington
B. R. Inman
James T. Lynn
Donald F. McHenry
Bruce K. MacLaury
Robert S. McNamara
Mary Patterson McPherson
Arjay Miller
Donald S. Perkins
J. Woodward Redmond
Charles W. Robinson
James D. Robinson III
Ralph S. Saul
Henry B. Schacht
Roger D. Semerad
Gerard C. Smith
Howard R. Swearer
Morris Tanenbaum
Phyllis A. Wallace
James D. Wolfensohn
Ezra K. Zilkha
Charles J. Zwick

Honorary Trustees
Eugene R. Black
Robert D. Calkins
Edward W. Carter
Bruce B. Dayton
Douglas Dillon
George M. Elsey
Huntington Harris
Roger W. Heyns
John E. Lockwood
William McC. Martin, Jr.
Herbert P. Patterson
H. Chapman Rose
Robert Brookings Smith
Sydney Stein, Jr.

THE BROOKINGS INSTITUTION is an independent organization devoted to nonpartisan research, education, and publication in economics, government, foreign policy, and the social sciences generally. Its principal purposes are to aid in the development of sound public policies and to promote public understanding of issues of national importance.

The Institution was founded on December 8, 1927, to merge the activities of the Institute for Government Research, founded in 1916, the Institute of Economics, founded in 1922, and the Robert Brookings Graduate School of Economics and Government, founded in 1924.

The Board of Trustees is responsible for the general administration of the Institution, while the immediate direction of the policies, program, and staff is vested in the President, assisted by an advisory committee of the officers and staff. The by-laws of the Institution state: "It is the function of the Trustees to make possible the conduct of scientific research, and publication, under the most favorable conditions, and to safeguard the independence of the research staff in the pursuit of their studies and in the publication of the results of such studies. It is not a part of their function to determine, control, or influence the conduct of particular investigations or the conclusions reached."

The President bears final responsibility for the decision to publish a manuscript as a Brookings book. In reaching his judgment on the competence, accuracy, and objectivity of each study, the President is advised by the director of the appropriate research program and weighs the views of a panel of expert outside readers who report to him in confidence on the quality of the work. Publication of a work signifies that it is deemed a competent treatment worthy of public consideration but does not imply endorsement of conclusions or recommendations.

The Institution maintains its position of neutrality on issues of public policy in order to safeguard the intellectual freedom of the staff. Hence interpretations or conclusions in Brookings publications should be understood to be solely those of the authors and should not be attributed to the Institution, to its trustees, officers, or other staff members, or to the organizations that support its research.

Foreword

COMMERCIAL BANK LENDING to developing countries, a thriving activity for most of the 1970s, underwent a critical reappraisal in the summer of 1982. The immediate trigger for the reappraisal was the difficulty experienced by Mexico in servicing its external debt. More fundamental causes were the world recession, the economic policies in some of the borrowing countries, and the lending policies of the commercial banks themselves. The "debt crisis," as it came to be called, sparked a variety of diagnoses and policy prescriptions. Among other things, the crisis induced the financial communities in the United States and the rest of the world to reexamine the structural soundness of international banking.

In this study, Jack M. Guttentag and Richard J. Herring focus on that controversial topic. They analyze the crisis in international lending and then offer their own set of proposals for addressing some of the problems. The authors also comment on recent changes in regulatory procedures adopted by the bank regulatory agencies in the United States in response to legislation passed by the U.S. Congress in the fall of 1983.

Guttentag and Herring presented a draft of their analysis and proposals at a workshop held at the Brookings Institution in January 1984. Their draft received a wide variety of comments, some supportive and some critical. Five of the participants in that workshop—William R. Cline, Donald J. Mathieson, Nicholas Sargen, Robert R. Bench, and C. Stewart Goddin—prepared written comments, which are included in the second part of this volume. The third part is an afterword by Guttentag and Herring that brings their views up to date and responds to the issues raised by the commentators.

The authors are faculty members at the Wharton School, the University of Pennsylvania, where Guttentag is the Robert Morris Professor of Banking and Herring is the director of the Wharton Program in International Banking and Finance. William R. Cline is a senior fellow at the Institute for International Economics in Washington, D.C. Donald J. Mathieson is acting chief of the Financial Studies Division in the Research Department of the International Monetary Fund. Nicholas Sargen is vice president, International Bond Market Research Division of Salomon Brothers in New York City. Robert R. Bench is deputy comptroller for international relations and financial evaluations, and C. Stewart Goddin is senior international economic adviser in the Economic and Policy Analysis Division, both at the Comptroller of the Currency, Washington, D.C.

Guttentag and Herring are grateful to Hans Angermueller, Peter Cooke, Raymond Dempsey, George von Furstenberg, Frederick Heldring, and Robert Mundheim for comments and suggestions. Charlotte Kaiser and Evelyn M. E. Taylor prepared the typescript. Karen J. Wirt edited the manuscript, Carolyn A. Rutsch verified its factual content, and Nancy Snyder did the proofreading.

The research for this study was carried out by the authors as part of an experimental study grant in international economic policy awarded to the Brookings Institution by the National Science Foundation. The views expressed here are those of the authors and the commentators and should not be attributed to the National Science Foundation or to the officers, trustees, or staff members of the Brookings Institution.

BRUCE K. MAC LAURY
President

January 1985
Washington, D.C.

Contents

The Current Crisis
in International Lending

INTERNATIONAL lending is currently in a state of crisis. The crisis has been managed until now by an ad hoc policy of "muddle through" in a gamble for time. This gamble is that the world economy will recover quickly and strongly enough to restore confidence in the debt-service ability of the major borrowing countries. The muddle-through policy consists of support from the International Monetary Fund (IMF), additional loans more or less coerced from creditor banks, and IMF conditions designed to restore creditworthiness.

The new loans, however, have been insufficient to prevent substantial reductions in per capita income in debtor countries, with a resulting buildup of strong social and political pressures not to comply with IMF conditions. Whether those pressures can be contained long enough for the adjustment policies adopted by the debtor countries, combined with world economic recovery, to restore financial health, no one knows. There is a high probability that the efforts to muddle through will fail. Something more is needed to deal with the current crisis. In addition, structural weaknesses that predispose international lending to crisis must be addressed.

These major structural weaknesses in international banking are summarized in the following section.[1] The next section describes the current crisis and the criteria that should be met by policies to deal with it. We then present a six-part proposal, which addresses both immediate needs and long-run structural reform. The last section evaluates new regulatory approaches to reform adopted by the three federal bank regulatory agencies as mandated by the International Lending Supervision Act of 1983.

---

1. See Jack M. Guttentag and Richard J. Herring, "Uncertainty and Insolvency Exposure by International Banks," Brookings Discussion Papers in International Economics 4 (Brookings, June 1983); and Guttentag and Herring, *The Lender-of-Last-Resort Function in an International Context,* Essays in International Finance 51 (Princeton University, Department of Economics, May 1983).

The policy proposals developed in this paper were presented at hearings before the Committee on Banking Finance and Urban Affairs of the U.S. House of Representatives on April 20, 1983.

Structural Weaknesses of International Lending

International lending tends to be a profitable activity during "normal" periods, which may extend for decades on end, but it is vulnerable to exceptionally heavy losses when a shock is produced by adverse events. This vulnerability is a consequence of several factors: a tendency to assume heavy concentrations of country-risk exposure, a high potential for the contagious transmission of shocks from one bank to another through the interbank market, and uncertainties about the availability of lender-of-last-resort facilities for some international banks and about the willingness of some parent banks to assume responsibility for their foreign affiliates.

International banks have sometimes behaved as if they suffer from "disaster myopia," that is, as if the probability of a major shock affecting their international loan portfolios were zero.[2] This is suggested by their willingness to lend amounts equal to a major portion of their capital to a single foreign country at interest rates that exceed the cost of funds (the "spread") by such small margins that any risk premiums included in the spreads must be extremely modest. It is also suggested by their willingness, except during crisis periods, to lend heavily at very narrow spreads to other international banks, some of which are not regulated, some of which have no assured lender of last resort, and some of which depend for their creditworthiness on legally ambiguous assurances of parental bank support.[3] Other evidence of disaster myopia is the willingness of these international banks to reduce their capacity to withstand major shocks during the 1970s when shock probabilities were rising.

International banks try to manage uncertainty by keeping their options open and by making only commitments that are revocable at short notice, including short-maturity lending.[4] This strategy of keeping maturities short, however, tends to make some banks feel more secure than they really are because the revocation of a commitment by one bank almost

2. This hypothesis is examined at greater length in Jack M. Guttentag and Richard J. Herring, "Commercial Bank Lending to Developing Countries: From Overlending to Underlending to Structural Reform," Brookings Discussion Papers in International Economics 16 (Brookings, June 1984).

3. For further discussion of this point, see Jack M. Guttentag and Richard Herring, "Prudential Aspects of the International Interbank Market," Brookings Discussion Papers in International Economics 17 (Brookings, July 1984).

4. For more details see Jack Guttentag and Richard Herring, "What Happens When Countries Cannot Pay Back Their Bank Loans? The Renegotiation Process," *Journal of Comparative Business and Capital Market Law*, vol. 5 (June 1983), pp. 209–31.

always shifts problems onto other banks. Short-maturity lending, furthermore, increases the potential for liquidity crises in the event of disturbances to confidence in a country's capacity to service its debts.

International banks also tend to herd by keeping their country exposures, capital ratios, and other measures of insolvency exposure in line with those of other international banks. This tactic minimizes vulnerability to criticism and increases the probability of government aid in the event of a crisis since the entire banking system will be in jeopardy, not just a single bank. Both herding and the policy of revocable commitments make banks more willing to assume heavy concentrations of country exposure.

Official supervisory agencies face special difficulties in constraining the tendency of international banks to assume excessive insolvency exposure. The bank supervisory process, as it has evolved over the decades, has focused on the current condition of banks and is not well designed to deal with exposure to major shocks of unknown probability. Supervisory authorities are also handicapped by problems in obtaining accurate and timely information about overseas activities of resident banks, by difficulties in preventing banks from overleveraging through foreign subsidiaries, and by competitive constraints on their freedom to impose prudential standards on the banks under their supervision that are more restrictive than those imposed on foreign banks.[5]

International banks are unable to control the total indebtedness of borrowing countries, and sometimes they do not even know what it is. When such countries succumb to the temptation to borrow too much, banks have no way of acting collectively to enforce restraint. It takes a crisis or near crisis for the banks to act jointly in a negotiation with the country to reschedule its debts, and only then does the IMF come into the picture to impose conditions for assistance.

The Debt Crisis and Policies to Alleviate It

The most important of the structural weaknesses implicated in the current crisis are the heavy concentrations of bank exposure to major borrow-

5. "Overleveraging" means reducing the ratio of capital to assets below some minimum established by the regulatory authority. If the regulator does not require the parent bank to consolidate its balance sheet with those of its subsidiaries, the parent bank may increase its effective leverage by operating through subsidiaries that are less well capitalized.

ers that are less developed countries, the absence of effective constraints on these countries before the emergence of crisis, and the heavy reliance by banks on short-term financing to protect themselves against change in the financial conditions of borrowers. During 1982 the debt-service capacity of these countries became strained by recession in the world economy while debt-service requirements rose markedly with higher world interest rates. The result was that confidence abruptly deteriorated and banks with maturing loans attempted to "run."

The remainder of the story has been well described by Richard S. Dale:

> Bank-lending to developing countries, which in recent years has been increasing at an annual rate of around 20 percent, came to an abrupt halt in the third quarter of last year as confidence evaporated in the wake of Mexico's financial collapse. This sudden interruption in the flow of credit threatened to precipitate multiple-country defaults since without new money the major borrowers could not be expected to pay interest, let alone principal, on their existing loans. In order to avert this danger, national authorities, in conjunction with the Bank for International Settlements and the International Monetary Fund, are orchestrating a series of emergency credit programs under which banks are being required to commit additional funds to problem borrowers according to a quota-allocation system which uses as its benchmark each bank's exposure to the country concerned. For the major borrowers, the annual increment has been set at around 7 percent of banks' outstanding loans, a figure that is intended to meet these countries' minimum external financing requirements while enabling banks to achieve a slight reduction in their country exposure relative to capital.[6]

The current arrangements constitute a system of coerced lending. Although the major banks are locked in by their heavy outstanding exposures, banks with less to lose have been "persuaded" to participate by major banks, central banks, and other official agencies.[7] A few have dragged their heels or refused to participate at all, although to date most have gone along.[8]

These current arrangements have achieved the pressing and immediate objective of keeping some amount of new credit flowing, but for how long

6. *International Financial Markets and Related Problems*, Hearings before the House Committee on Banking Finance and Urban Affairs, 98 Cong. 1 sess. (Government Printing Office, 1983), p. 375.

7. For an analysis of the ways in which decisions on new loans are affected by outstanding exposures, see Guttentag and Herring, "Uncertainty and Insolvency Exposure."

8. In private discussions two banks related to us that they had unilaterally recalculated their required contributions to the Mexican pool basing their exposure on a different ("fairer") date than the one specified, and using a different ("fairer") definition of exposure. They encountered no opposition, although their new loans were significantly reduced. Some Swiss and German banks have reportedly resisted participation strongly.

nobody knows. If prospects for a resumption of orderly debt-service payments do not improve, the smaller banks that tend to have less exposure relative to capital may refuse to participate in new loans. In the aggregate the nine major U.S. money-center banks account for about three-fifths of total exposure of U.S. banks to Mexico, Brazil, and Argentina; the next fifteen largest banks account for about one-fifth; and the remaining banks (several hundred), about one-fifth. If the last group drops out, the capacity of the larger banks to pick up the slack is open to question. Even if they do, the consequence will be an exacerbation of the already excessive concentration of exposure among a small group of banks.

Coerced lending is a response to the exigencies of the moment: (1) the need for troubled debtor countries not only to rollover their outstanding indebtedness to international banks but also to increase debt in order to avoid politically destabilizing reductions in their aggregate demand and a further weakening of the world economy; (2) the inadequacy of the resources of the IMF to finance stabilization policies in the troubled debtor countries; (3) the financial impossibility of paying off the banks that do not want to rollover their claims on troubled debtor countries; and (4) the political necessity of not appearing to bail out banks.

Coerced lending, however, has not provided any net cash flows to troubled debtor countries, and does not resolve the basic structural problems in international banking that contributed to the debt crisis. What is needed is a dependable method of increasing the volume of loans in the short run that is consistent with and contributes to long-run structural reform.

A breakdown of existing arrangements would have severe worldwide repercussions. Some of these repercussions might be softened by actions of Western governments to assist borrowing countries, banks, or both, but such actions would themselves have enormous economic and political costs. The abrupt cessation of new loans to major developing country borrowers would cause a drastic reduction of aggregate demand in countries that have relied heavily on external finance. This shock could have painful consequences for the United States and other developed countries in several dimensions. The abrupt decline in living standards could destabilize political relationships. The demand for exports from developed countries would fall sharply. And a sizable write-off of loans would markedly reduce the stated capital of the leading international banks and cause a serious shortfall in the availability of bank credit. The resulting deflationary drag on the world economy could abort the emerging recovery.

Policies to deal with the current debt crisis must thus meet the following short-run objectives:

It is vitally necessary to keep money flowing, for as long as necessary, to debtor countries that are meeting the performance criteria negotiated in standby agreements with the IMF. The means for doing this should distinguish temporary liquidity problems that require only temporary assistance from longer-run structural problems that might require subsidies. Agencies providing assistance with the temporary problems are often referred to as "lenders of last resort."[9] At the outset the presumption should be that the problems are temporary and require only lender-of-last-resort assistance.

It is equally necessary to reduce cash-flow burdens on debtor countries having payment difficulties. The means for doing this should discourage countries from soliciting special assistance when they do not require it.

The policies chosen must be politically feasible, which means that they cannot involve large subsidies from governments. Subsidies will not become feasible unless there is a disaster, and a disaster is what such policies seek to prevent.

The policies should provide a method of cushioning the impact of the shock on bank balance sheets if the condition of debtor countries does not improve and large losses must be taken.

It is also very important that short-run measures should be consistent with long-run structural reforms. Such reforms should meet two major objectives.

They should provide external control over a borrowing country so that constraints arise before a crisis develops. These constraints should operate on both sides of the market, that is, they should discourage imprudent borrowing and lending.

These policies should reduce, or at least not aggravate, the banks' existing concentrations of country-risk exposure relative to bank capital.

A Six-Part Proposal

The proposals advanced here to alleviate the debt crisis fall into six parts, three short-run and three long-run.

---

9. For discussion of the classical role of the lender of last resort, see Guttentag and Herring, *The Lender-of-Last-Resort Function*.

New Marketable Perpetuals Certificates with Prior Claim

The first proposal is addressed to the problem of keeping money flowing to countries with debt-service problems. Operationally the trigger is the occurrence of arrearages in government, government-guaranteed external debt, or both, followed by the negotiation of a standby agreement with the IMF for a drawing against the country's quota in excess of the first credit tranche.[10] The preconditions, performance criteria, and policy understandings negotiated with the IMF in the development of an adjustment program as part of a standby agreement would provide the external controls needed to implement the proposal.

The new money required by the country would be raised through the issuance of marketable, floating rate certificates that never mature ("perpetuals"), and these certificates would have a prior claim over all old debt. Each issue of perpetuals would be approved by the IMF, and a portion of it would be acquired as an investment either by the IMF or the International Bank for Reconstruction and Development (World Bank). A sharing clause would require that all holders are treated equally. Direct control over new issues and surveillance by the IMF would continue until the perpetuals have been retired.

This scheme formalizes a LIFO rule (last in first out) for the treatment of creditors. In contrast, debtors experiencing payment problems could use a FIFO rule (first in first out), which has the advantage of apparent fairness. A FIFO rule, however, discourages new lending because new loans automatically go to the end of the repayment queue. A LIFO rule has the crucial advantage that it encourages new lending, but it raises an issue of credibility. Formalization of the LIFO rule, and the involvement and control exercised by the IMF, would eliminate or substantially reduce the risk that the new, prior-claim certificates would themselves be subordinated in the future.

This proposal meets the primary objective of increasing the control over the flow of credit. The proposal offers essentially a carrot rather than a stick to induce lenders to participate. Because the perpetuals have a superior claim over old debt and some of the perpetuals would be held by the IMF or the World Bank, they would be regarded as a prime instrument by

10. For a lucid explanation of the mechanics of borrowing from the IMF and the negotiation of conditionality, see John Williamson, "The Lending Policies of the International Monetary Fund," Institute for International Economics, Policy Analysis in International Economics 1 (August 1982).

new investors. For the same reason, instead of aggravating the existing concentration of exposure, the perpetuals would constitute a step in the reverse direction.

The ability to authorize issues of perpetuals should also give the IMF greater clout with large debtor countries. Debtor countries might be more willing to submit to an IMF stabilization program if they were confident that sufficient financing would be available for the duration of that program. Moreover, in some instances stabilization programs might be better suited to the needs of the borrowing country. The fundamental rationale for providing financial assistance during a stabilization program is that long-run elasticities are higher than short-run elasticities. If a larger volume of new loans allowed the adjustment to be extended over a longer period of time, it would be less painful for the debtor country and less disruptive for the debtor country's trade partners and the world economy.

This proposal, together with the next one, would sharply reduce the cash-flow burden on the debtor country by eliminating concern about repayment of principal. Debt service henceforth—so long as the control procedures remain in force—would consist of interest payments only. Paradoxically, because of the incentive for a country to retire new perpetuals as soon as possible to avoid supervision by the IMF, the perpetuals could well have short lives.

Transforming Old Government Debt into Subordinated Perpetuals

The second proposal is addressed to the problem of reducing debt-service burdens and pertains to the treatment of the "old," or existing, government debt of countries that meet the trigger conditions specified above. A major portion of the old debt would be purchased by a sovereign entity of that country (in most cases the appropriate institution being the central bank), which in payment would issue an equivalent amount of floating rate perpetuals certificates—one issue for each currency in which the country had external debt.[11] All the old debt denominated in a given currency would therefore be homogenized and would carry a single interest rate spread. This would be a penalty spread set at the highest level of any of the old spreads, and perhaps a little higher. Private debt would be left for negotiations between lenders and borrowers in each case. In general we believe that the subordinated debt treated in this way should be

11. For convenience these are referred to as "old" subordinated perpetuals to distinguish them from the new, prior-claim perpetuals proposed above.

limited to that owed or guaranteed by the government, although the exact details of the coverage might differ for each country.

This proposal reduces the liquidity burden on the debtor country by eliminating the need to repay the principal, but increases the real debt burden because of the penalty interest rate. It is thus akin to lender-of-last-resort assistance in that it presumes long-run solvency, although the assistance is sufficiently burdensome that the borrower has strong incentives to repay as soon as possible. Thus there are no attractions for borrowers who do not really need debt-service relief.

Treating old debt in this way avoids the distortion of incentives, the inequities, and the thorny political issues that subsidies entail. It is inefficient and inequitable to allocate foreign aid preferentially to the countries that have been the largest borrowers. Such a policy only encourages imprudent future borrowing. Although at some point the issue of forgiveness of debt may have to be faced, it is prudent to defer it until a careful assessment can be made of the borrower's debt-service capacity. The allocation of foreign aid should not be determined by the exigencies of meeting a liquidity crisis.

If a country's problems prove to be temporary, it would retire the new certificates while staying current on the old ones. Having again become creditworthy, the country would gradually retire the old certificates to reduce its debt burden with proceeds of refinancings in the market. Under the most favorable scenario the old certificates could rise in value above par and thus provide incentives for sale by bank holders. Less favorable scenarios cover a wide range of possibilities from faithful servicing of the old debt but with little prospect for redemption to partial, intermittent, or delayed servicing, to de facto repudiation.

Implementation of proposals regarding new and old certificates requires the concurrence of the banks holding the old loans. The banks would of course be happy to be free of providing new credits to troubled countries but would not want to have their old claims subordinated and converted into perpetuals. Nevertheless, a good case can be made that the banks would be substantially better off under our proposed arrangements than under the present system of coerced lending. If the debtor countries did not recover, the banks would lose in either case; but under the proposed arrangements the countries would have incentives and opportunities to restore their debt-service capacity. In the last analysis a key factor determining whether the banks emerge whole is whether the troubled debtors perceive that their interest lies in servicing their old debt.

We view the implementation procedure as proceeding separately for each country in trouble. Each case requires agreement between the banks, the IMF, and the debtor country. Negotiations must include old debt that is converted into perpetuals certificates, treatment of unconverted old debt, amount and timing of new issues of certificates, amount of direct assistance by the IMF, and conditions imposed by the IMF. The proposed arrangements should be viewed as a general framework within which specific agreements would be hammered out to meet the requirements of specific cases.

Valuation of Old Debt

To meet the objective of cushioning shocks to bank balance sheets in the event that large losses must be taken, an administrative policy is proposed for adjusting the value of perpetuals on the books of bank holders: if the country remains current on its interest payments, banks can continue to carry them at face value. For every month that interest is delinquent the value must be written down by 1 percent. If a country paid no interest at all, the payments would be fully written off in 100 months.

The proposed valuation rule requires that if a country does not stay current on the old debt, the banks immediately begin a valuation adjustment. By design, the adjustment would not correspond exactly to changes in true market values. If a writedown caused book values to fall below market values, which could happen if the country allowed arrears to develop and then began faithfully to pay, the banks could realize a capital gain by selling, which could enhance exposure diversification. If—to take the worst case—market values plummeted to zero because the country repudiated its old debt, the writedown policy would cushion the shock to bank balance sheets.[12] This would not fool equity holders or bank creditors

---

12. Lord Lever proposes a much more complicated procedure for allowing banks to stretch their losses. He suggests "the central bank . . . offer to discount the paper of the private banks and to roll over interest and repayments to match any defaults or delays by the borrowers. This would be matched by a commitment from the private banks to make provision out of their profits over a long period for the loans on which there had been default or where payment had been delayed. . . . The arrangement would sustain the banks by enabling them greatly to extend the period required to make provision for their questionable loans without calling their liquidity or solvency into question." Because the banks in this scheme must ultimately redeem at face value all the paper discounted with the central bank, the procedure accomplishes no more than the simple writedown policy proposed above. See Harold Lever, "International Banking's House of Cards," *New York Times*, September 24, 1982.

but would provide regulators with leeway to allow banks time for rebuilding their capital.[13]

Under the existing system of coerced lending, formulation of a general writedown policy is immobilized by the new loan requirements. It is not feasible to ask banks to increase their exposures to a country in trouble and simultaneously to write off a portion of the same loans.

Proposals for Long-run Reform: Mark to Market

The principal long-run objective in international lending is to establish a mechanism that constrains both banks and borrowing countries well before debt levels become excessive. The fourth proposal is to have bank regulatory agencies require that all cross-border loans periodically be marked to market; balance sheet values would be adjusted to conform to market values. Another source of constraint, associated with disclosure of information on country exposures of individual banks, is discussed below.

Mark-to-market accounting encounters two standard objections. The first is that if it is a good idea it should be applied universally, not just to foreign assets. The second is that for many assets the proposal is very difficult to implement because of the absence of reliable market value data. Both these objections are well taken. We believe that, in principle, balance sheets should be marked to market in toto, but because of the implementation costs involved it is not worthwhile except in special cases in which the potential benefits are especially compelling.[14] Foreign lending is one such special case. Mark-to-market accounting for foreign assets would impose badly needed constraints on the behavior of both lenders and borrowers for which there have not been any adequate substitutes.

Under mark-to-market accounting banks would exercise greater restraint in lending to debtor countries at an early stage. Disaster myopia is encouraged by current procedures under which writeoffs of loans to a

---

13. Regulatory decisions on whether to terminate a bank and, if so, whether to accomplish this through liquidation, merger, or some sort of takeover are based on the firm's book net worth, not its true net worth. A firm that is forced to take losses in excess of its book net worth is technically insolvent and subject to termination, even though it may have positive true net worth associated with its going value of concern. For more discussion see Jack Guttentag and Richard Herring, "The Insolvency of Financial Institutions: Assessment and Regulatory Disposition," in Paul Wachtel, ed., *Crisis in the Economic and Financial Structure* (Lexington Books, 1982), pp. 99–126.

14. For a discussion of marking balance sheets to market in toto see Guttentag and Herring, "The Insolvency of Financial Institutions."

country experiencing payment problems can be delayed more or less indefinitely. Indefinite delays can be rationalized because there is always some chance that the debtor country may be able to meet the rescheduled payments. If these loans are periodically marked to market, however, banks must anticipate that writeoffs will occur as expectations regarding repayment prospects deteriorate.[15] Hence rate spreads will rise to reflect the perceived risk that payments may not be made on schedule.

When countries begin to embark on imprudent programs, furthermore, banks will have greater incentive to say no. Under existing arrangements banks are too easily persuaded to go along, especially when there is heavy exposure. The tendency of banks to evaluate the performance of lending officers over short time horizons and high mobility among these officers contributes to a willingness to allow country borrowers to drift along rather than to take the painful measures required to restore payments equilibrium.

A mark-to-market policy would strengthen the negotiating stance of banks in this position. Assuming the market is well informed, a portion of outstanding loans will already have been marked down, and new loans that are not accompanied by substantial constructive changes in the borrower's macroeconomic and development policies will drop in value as soon as they are disbursed. There would be little point in extending new loans that serve only to delay the adjustment process.

Countries pursuing imprudent policies will be pressed to change their policies earlier not only because bank resistance would grow sooner but also because of the direct impact of changes in market values on the policymaking process within the borrowing country. A decline in market value in anticipation of future economic trouble would constitute tangible and public evidence of the market's lack of confidence in the borrowing country's policies. This would place the architects of imprudent policies on the defensive and strengthen the hand of their opponents.

A mark-to-market policy would also make it easier for bank creditors and equity holders to assess how a bank's condition is being affected by its position in foreign loans. To be useful for this purpose, a mark-to-market policy should be accompanied by the disclosure of country exposures by individual banks, a proposal discussed below.

A mark-to-market policy could be disruptive if it were adopted at a time when large disparities existed between book and market values. Under

15. For an explicit expression describing the valuation of foreign loans, see Guttentag and Herring, "What Happens When Countries Cannot Pay Back Their Bank Loans."

Table 1. Adjusted Total Margin over LIBOR of Nafinsa Floating Rate Notes, January 1981 through March 1983
Basis points

Period	Average	High	Low
January 9, 1981, to November 13, 1981	43.5	68.7	15.8
November 20, 1981, to January 15, 1982	75.8	81.8	69.4
January 22, 1982, to June 4, 1982	112.1	119.5	93.3
June 11, 1982, to June 25, 1982	168.8	169.3	168.0
July 2, 1982, to October 1, 1982	n.a.	n.a.	n.a.
October 8, 1982, to March 18, 1983	927.2	964.3	895.7

Source: Derived from unpublished data provided by Salomon Brothers.
n.a. Not available. No observations during this period. See text discussion.

such circumstances, some type of administered phase-in policy, such as the proposed rule of 1 percent a month discussed above, would be useful.

The beneficial effects of a mark-to-market policy presuppose some degree of prescience on the part of markets in anticipating payment difficulties. To assess the validity of this supposition we drew upon Salomon Brothers data that show weekly quotations on floating rate notes of Nacional Financiera, S.A. (Nafinsa), the huge Mexican government-owned credit institution. With a few exceptions, the quotations are weekly and reflect actual transactions within the week. Table 1 shows averages of weekly interest rate spreads over the London Interbank Offered Rate (LIBOR) in basis points per year for selected periods during 1981–83.[16] Figure 1 presents weekly observations for these data.[17]

On August 20, 1982, the Mexican government telexed banks around the world announcing its inability to meet its upcoming debt-service obligation. Obviously this problem did not arise overnight. When did the market for Nafinsa notes recognize that conditions were deteriorating?

16. The spread is what Salomon Brothers calls the "adjusted total margin" over LIBOR because it takes account of not only the contractual coupon spread and current price of the note, but also accrued interest and the expected price adjustment as the note approaches the coupon rate reset date. For a more detailed description, see Jeffrey Hanna and Felicia Freed, "Eurodollar Floating Rate Notes: Part II, Techniques for Assessing Relative Value" (Salomon Brothers, January 1982).

17. During the turbulent period from July through September 1982, Salomon Brothers did not record any transactions.

Figure 1. Adjusted Total Margin over LIBOR of Nafinsa Floating Rate Notes, Based on Observations from January 9, 1981, through March 18, 1982[a]

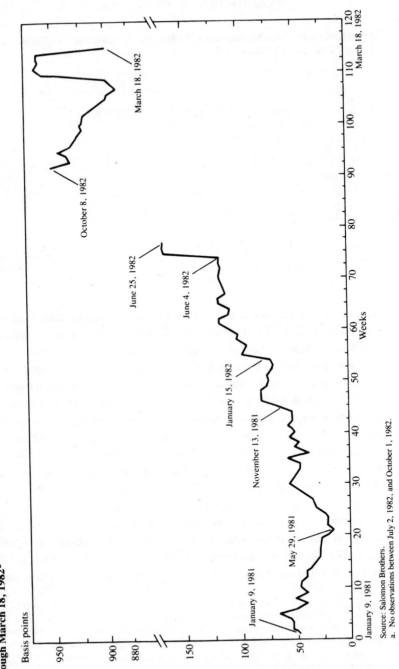

Source: Salomon Brothers.
a. No observations between July 2, 1982, and October 1, 1982.

From the figure it could have been as early as May 1981, since spreads trended up slowly between May and November. This is not conclusive because the rise was erratic and did not bring the level of spreads above those that had prevailed at times before May 1981. The evidence is very clear, however, that by November the market was reacting to indications of bad news. During the nine weeks ending January 15, 1982, the average spread jumped to 75.8 basis points from 42.4 over the previous eleven months. During the succeeding six months, the average was 112.1 points, and during the last three weeks of June it was 168.8 points. At that point the market ceased to function and no trades were executed. When the market resumed in October 1982 the spread was over 900 points.[18]

Thus it is clear that the market had misgivings about Mexico at least as early as the last quarter of 1981 and that the market readings became progressively worse during 1982. If a mark-to-market policy had been in effect, alarm bells would have gone off well before the crisis hit. It should be emphasized, furthermore, that this early warning occurred within the context of very incomplete data available on the condition of Mexico's finances. Greater market efficiency may result when better data become available.

A mark-to-market policy requires a market. Other valuation procedures are possible, but a reliable secondary market is best. And the market must cover claims at least similar to those held in the portfolios being valued. An effective market would also provide a mechanism for diversifying ownership of loans to debtor countries, the second major objective of long-run reform.

Creating a Secondary Market

The process through which private capital has been transferred from surplus to deficit countries since World War II is, in an important sense, at the opposite pole from the process in effect during the 1920s. In the earlier period banks acted as facilitators and brokers in the transfer of bonds to the public and to nonbank institutional investors, the latter including their own trust departments. Because the main interest of the banks was in the fees and other income they earned (either directly or indirectly) from bond placements, it was sometimes alleged that their concern about the creditworthiness of individual borrowers and about country risk was not very

18. The Mexican government has continued to make the interest payments on its floating rate notes.

great. While the collapse of the foreign bond market in the 1930s was hardly the result of poor bond underwriting, the role of the banks in the process clearly involved serious conflicts of interest that might have resulted in creation of excessive debt and subsequent widespread defaults even if there had not been a major depression. The key factor underlying the conflict of interest was that banks were strategically situated to assess credit risk but they assumed little or no risk themselves. In contrast, since World War II commercial banks have assumed *all* the credit risk, their portfolios have become increasingly unbalanced, and there is no effective means for spreading the risk more evenly among smaller banks, nonbank institutions, or the public.

In cases in which banks are heavily exposed to a given country or countries, they have not had incentives to sell loans to others. When loans are in good standing, they are worth more to the originating banks than to any potential buyers, who would fear that the originating banks would sell their least desirable loans. To protect themselves, such buyers would feel obliged to incur significant costs in obtaining information about the loans. When doubts arise about whether loans from a given country will be serviced on schedule, the originating banks might like to sell them. Under those circumstances, however, buyers would require a very substantial discount if they were willing to buy them at all, and the banks would take a loss. Because the originating banks can usually avoid taking a loss indefinitely by renegotiating foreign loans, they prefer to hold them. Thus most of the time foreign loans are worth more to the originating bank than to others if the loans are in good standing, and also if they are not.

A limited type of secondary market in country loans has developed recently as a result of pressures on large originating banks to avoid further increases in exposures.[19] In some cases, sales have been prompted by liquidity pressures on banks whose headquarters are in countries with payment difficulties. Transactions in this type of market are called "subparticipations" because the seller usually retains title to the loan and the borrower is not aware of the transaction. Because of this, the market operates in something of a sub-rosa atmosphere.

The subparticipation market is basically a relationship market in which transactions are made directly between banks that do other types of business with each other, and to a degree the buying bank must trust the selling

---

19. This description draws heavily on Charles Grant, "A Boom in Broking Out Loans," *Euromoney* (November 1982), pp. 37–41.

bank not to "dump" questionable loans on it.[20] The legal status of the buyer in the event of a loan restructuring may be tenuous, and the documentation defining the rights and duties of buyer and seller varies from case to case. This type of market does not provide a source of reliable data on market value because every transaction is more or less unique. Nor does it provide a mechanism by which investors other than banks actively engaged in international banking can buy and sell foreign loans.

A secondary market mechanism is needed that is open and above board, one in which the instruments traded fall into a limited number of homogeneous categories; it should employ standardized documents and be attractive to investors of any type. Such a mechanism should enable banks to take advantage of their investment in capacity to originate foreign loans, based mainly on information and information sources. It should also leave intact the self-interest of loan originators in carefully controlling and monitoring loan risk. A return to the system of the 1920s, in which the banks shifted most or all of the exposure to others, is not what is needed.

The proposal advanced above to create a new, prior-claim certificate for countries having debt-service problems and to homogenize their outstanding externally held public debt would constitute an important step toward the development of effective secondary markets. In general, a large volume of homogeneous instruments encourages the development of market facilities, although markets do not always develop. Even if markets did arise, they would only cover the debt of countries experiencing payment difficulties. New institutional arrangements are needed that would generate value data covering the external debt of all borrowing countries, not just those in trouble.

After examining a variety of approaches to this problem we have concluded that the most promising is to have the IMF, the World Bank, or a new entity assume a conduit role by buying loans, pooling them, and selling participation interests in the pools. A model for this type of market is provided in the United States by the Federal Home Loan Mortgage Corporation, a quasi-government agency that developed an efficient secondary market in conventional home mortgages. Its model has since been followed, with minor adjustments, by some strictly private conduit firms.

20. One banker is quoted as saying "No bank worth its name would dump junk. I recall that one bank sold off some assets of a certain country just before that country rescheduled. There followed such a furore in the market, that the vendor was forced to buy back the assets to protect its name" (ibid., p. 41).

The main functions of a new conduit organization are briefly described as follows.

The conduit buys loans from those who originate them now (commercial banks), or from others who might enter the business. The existence of a secondary market eliminates the need to finance new loans permanently, and thereby encourages the development of loan origination specialists.

The conduit establishes the legal and accounting systems and procedures necessary to pool a number of purchased loans to a given country in a given currency and issues certificates representing undivided participation interests in the entire pool. It also determines the form of the certificates, including rate, denomination, maturity, principal repayment schedule if any, mode of sale, custody and delivery of documents, and so on.

Eligibility requirements are defined by the conduit for the loans it will buy. These requirements are based on the needs of the investors to whom participation interests are sold and perhaps on public policy objectives.[21] For example, an international conduit might refuse to purchase short-maturity loans of a given country if it viewed the outstanding volume of such loans as excessive.

The conduit establishes servicing obligations, including warranties or coinsurance by loan sellers, to assure their interest in originating good loans and in maintaining proper surveillance over old ones.

The conduit, as any prudent lender, defines eligibility requirements for borrowers and formalizes them for use by the originating lenders.

Information requirements for borrowers are also defined. In the residential mortgage market in which the number of borrowers is much larger than the number of lenders, information on borrowers is collected by the lender for transmission to the conduit. In international markets, however, the number of lenders is larger than the number of borrowers, so that it would be more efficient for the conduit itself to collect information on the borrower. An international conduit would no doubt require data on total indebtedness, the maturity structure of indebtedness, and other important features of a country's financial status as a condition for purchasing its

---

21. Investors will be indifferent to the characteristics of the loans in the pool only if the certificates issued against the pool carry full insurance by a completely credible insurer. For further discussion of this and other aspects of conduit operations, see Jack M. Guttentag, "The Conventional Passthrough Market: Trickle or Flood?" in Federal Home Loan Bank of San Francisco, *Savings and Loan Asset Management under Deregulation* (San Francisco FHLB, 1980), pp. 271–313; and Guttentag, "Mortgage Passthroughs: Structure and Policy" (Washington, D.C.: Mortgage Insurance Companies of America, 1982).

paper. Unless the conduit provides extensive guarantees to investors, this information on borrowers would have to be provided to investors.

The conduit sets up a marketing system for selling the certificates. This could range from self-administered auctions, to over-the-counter sales through branches of cooperating banks, to large underwritings by major investment banking houses.

Some guarantees may be provided by the conduit to the certificate holders, ranging from reimbursement for losses in the event of misfeasance by the servicing agent to guaranteeing absolutely the timely payment of interest and principal. More extensive guarantees increase the attractiveness of the certificates, which in turn increases the conduit's leverage in setting loan and borrower eligibility requirements. Extensive guarantees offered by an international conduit, however, would require the contingent financial backing of major countries.

The conduit also makes a market for its certificates, or arranges for others to do so. (Dealer firms make a secondary market for participation certificates of the Federal Home Loan Mortgage Corporation.)

In summary, the basic function of the conduit is instrument transformation. It purchases an asset, transforms it, and sells it at a higher price. The transformed instrument offers greater marketability and security than the original instrument; it may have some guarantees provided by the conduit; and it is also less costly to own because servicing and recordkeeping are done by others. The price spread reflects these advantages, and it must be large enough to cover the conduit's expenses and provide an adequate return on its capital.[22]

The more guarantees the conduit offers on its certificates, the larger the price spread is, but more guarantees also raise the amount of capital or other support required. Important guarantees offered to certificate holders that are credibly supported by the conduit's capital provide the conduit

---

22. In an early comment on our proposal, George von Furstenberg argued that "secondary markets do not function well in areas in which trust, reputation and related perceptions are so important to assessing loan quality and prospects." See George von Furstenberg, "Comment on Guttentag and Herring," in M. Wachter and S. Wachter, eds., *Removing Obstacles to Economic Growth* (University of Pennsylvania Press, 1984), p. 417. While it is true that conduit markets to date have been developed (by design) with very low-risk instruments, there is no inherent reason that they cannot operate effectively with high-risk instruments. The successful development of mutual funds in low-grade bonds as well as active auction markets in highly volatile common stocks suggests that the key to marketability is transaction volume and homogeneity rather than risk.

with maximum clout in imposing loan and borrower eligibility require-ments.[23]

The economic feasibility of conduit operations is also affected by the underlying demand for ownership transfers. We have argued that the development of a secondary market in country loans would facilitate diversification of country loan exposure across institutions and individ-uals, but it is also true that an increased demand for diversification by heavily exposed lenders would increase the demand for conduit services. This would also happen if regulators imposed country exposure limits on banks that were lower than the levels now prevailing.

We see the basic role of the conduit as providing a market in loans for countries in good standing. It seems reasonable that a conduit might also make a market in prior-claim perpetuals and old (subordinated) perpetuals certificates of countries experiencing payment difficulties if secondary markets in these instruments are otherwise slow to develop.

Disclosure of Detailed Data on Country Exposure

We have argued elsewhere that because bank regulators have been unable to constrain increasing concentrations of country-risk exposure among the largest international banks, they should release detailed data on country exposure to the market.[24] Disclosure of country exposure data on individual banks would permit bank creditors and equity holders to moni-tor such risks more effectively.

How effective the monitoring would be, however, is another question. Market-imposed constraints on imprudent country borrowers are quite different from market constraints on bank exposure to country risk. A well-informed market will react immediately to perceptions of overbor-rowing or imprudent macroeconomic or development policies, as the mar-ket did in the case of the Nafinsa notes. But it is not clear that markets will

23. We do not envisage the conduit providing guarantees against loss associated with borrower default because the capital or other support required would be enormous. It is appropriate, however, for a conduit to provide guarantees regarding procedural matters—for example, guarantees that the loans it purchases have met the standards the conduit has established, that documentation is complete and correct, that loan servicing is adequately performed and loan payments properly escrowed, and so forth.

24. See Jack Guttentag and Richard Herring, "Public Policy toward International Bank-ing," in Carole Kitti and Alan Rapoport, eds., *International Economic Policy: A Collo-quium on Phase I Research Findings* (Washington, D.C.: National Science Foundation, 1982), pp. I-35 to I-67.

react to constrain bank exposures to a given country before evidence surfaces that the country is in difficulty. Markets as well as banks can suffer from disaster myopia. Although most of the special factors noted earlier that encourage disaster myopia by banks do not apply to the open market, without better evidence than is now at hand, we cannot be sure in advance that disclosure will constrain banks at a sufficiently early stage to be effective. For this reason, we also remain noncommittal about the possible need to set country loan limits in the future.[25]

The Regulatory Approach

A comprehensive set of proposals for dealing with the debt crisis has emerged from the regulatory-legislative process in the United States. Following the crisis, three U.S. federal bank regulatory agencies—the Federal Deposit Insurance Corporation, the Office of the Comptroller of the Currency, and the Board of Governors of the Federal Reserve System—suddenly found themselves under intense political pressure to "crack down" on the banks; at the same time they were encouraging banks to make new loans in support of the IMF stabilization programs and were attempting to persuade Congress to sanction an increase in the IMF quota of the United States. An adequately "tough" regulatory response in effect became a political quid pro quo for increasing the IMF quota. The result was the joint memorandum of the three agencies of April 7, 1983, which was a heroic attempt to respond constructively to political pressures by remedying acknowledged weaknesses in regulatory controls in ways that did not interfere with restructuring programs, while deflecting more extreme proposals for disciplining the banks.

The effort was largely successful. The substantive portions of the IMF bill applying to international banking that ultimately emerged after a difficult political struggle follow closely the original recommendations of the regulatory agencies.[26] Congressional proponents of more extreme measures had to settle for ideological rhetoric with little significant force—

25. The three federal regulatory agencies have been opposed to detailed disclosures of country exposures and to country loan limits—until very recently, when they suddenly relented under intense congressional pressure to "do something," and came out in favor of disclosure, while remaining adament against loan limits. See joint memorandum, C. T. Conover, William M. Isaac, and Paul A. Volcker to Fernand J. St Germain, "Program for Improved Supervision of International Lending," April 7, 1983.

26. Title IX, 97 Stat. 1278, International Lending Supervision Act of 1983.

such as requiring the secretary of the treasury to instruct the U.S. executive director of the IMF to "work for" lower interest rates and longer maturities on international loans or to oppose using IMF funds to bail out banks. The remainder of this paper evaluates the substantive sections of this act, most of which have been implemented by the regulatory agencies. The primary thrust of the act is to "assure that the economic health and stability of the United States and the other nations of the world shall not be adversely affected or threatened in the future by imprudent lending practices or inadequate supervision."[27] In line with this thrust, our evaluation focuses mainly on long-run implications.

Reserve and Loan Classification

Among the important issues that have arisen in the wake of the debt crisis is the accounting treatment of loans to countries having payment difficulties. The accounting problem is complex because a number of objectives are involved in determining an appropriate set of policies and the objectives are not necessarily consistent.

From an accountant's standpoint, a basic objective is accuracy in measuring the true condition of a bank. There is so much uncertainty in connection with the "true value" of some country loans, however, that variance in well-informed judgments is bound to be very wide.[28] From a supervisory standpoint, accuracy may be counterproductive in the short run if it forces bank supervisors to take actions that are not in the public interest such as terminating a bank that could resolve its problems in time.

From an investor's standpoint it is important that accounting rules be applied consistently across banks so that reported balance sheets and income statements are comparable. Our discussions with bankers suggest that writeoff policies at different banks are based more heavily on the extent of the individual bank's exposure and on its current earnings—the lower its exposure and the higher its earnings, the more likely is a writeoff—than on an assessment of the debt-service prospects of the borrowing country.[29] The new policies discussed below largely accomplish the

27. 12 U.S.C. 3901.

28. For a discussion of a variety of approaches to valuing loans that generate different results, see Colin Brown, "The Problem of Provisions against Sovereign Debt," *The Banker* (February 1983).

29. A bank regulator in a country that closely monitors writeoff policies related to us the details of a negotiation with a major international bank. In substance, according to the regulator, the bank determined writeoffs as a residual, equal to the bank's current income less dividends and "necessary" increases in reserves.

consistency objective for U.S. banks, although noncomparability with foreign banks remains.[30]

In a crisis situation it is important that the accounting treatment of old loans encourages banks to behave constructively in restructuring such loans and in renegotiating new loans. This also can conflict with the objective of balance sheet accuracy.

In the long run, accounting policies should encourage banks to exercise restraint in exposing themselves to country risk if other restraints are weak or lacking, as has been the case.

During February 1984 the three federal banking agencies implemented a provision of the International Lending Supervision Act that requires banks to establish a special Allocated Transfer Risk Reserve (ATRR) against certain categories of international assets. The establishment of an ATRR would depend on:

(A) Whether the quality of a banking institution's assets has been impaired by a protracted inability of public or private obligors in a foreign country to make payments on their external indebtedness as indicated by such factors, among others, as whether: (1) Such obligors have failed to make full interest payments on external indebtedness; (2) Such obligors have failed to comply with the terms of any restructured indebtedness; or (3) A foreign country has failed to comply with any International Monetary Fund or other suitable adjustment program; or

(B) Whether no definite prospects exist for the orderly restoration of debt service.[31]

The ATRR is charged against current income and is not considered as part of capital and surplus or allowances for possible loan losses for regulatory, supervisory, or disclosure purposes. The initial year's provision for the ATRR is 10 percent of the principal amount of each specified international asset "or such greater or lesser percentage determined by the Federal banking agencies. Additional provision, if any, for the ATRR in subsequent years shall be 15 percent of the principal amount of each specified international asset, or such greater or lesser percentage determined by the Federal banking agencies."[32]

The new requirement is tied to a new classification system, adopted by the three agencies in September 1983, for loans adversely affected by transfer risk. The categories are as follows:

I. *Substandard:* (1) A country is not complying with its external service obligations, as evidenced by arrearages, forced restructuring, or rollovers; and (2) the

---

30. For a discussion of how rules differ among countries see Geoffrey Bell and Graeme Rutledge, "How to Account for Problem Loans," *Euromoney* (January 1984), pp. 43–46.

31. *Federal Register,* vol. 49 (February 13, 1984), p. 5591.

32. Ibid.

country is not in the process of adopting an IMF or other suitable economic adjustment program, or is not adequately adhering to such a program; or (3) the country and its bank creditors have not negotiated a viable rescheduling and are unlikely to do so in the near future.

II. *Value impaired:* A country has protracted arrearages, as indicated by more than one of the following: the country has not fully paid its interest for six months; the country has not complied with IMF programs (and there is no immediate prospect for compliance); the country has not met rescheduling terms for over one year; the country shows no definite prospects for an orderly restoration of debt service in the near future.

III. *Loss:* This category applies when the loan is considered uncollectible and of such little value that its continuance as a bankable asset is not warranted. An example would be an outright statement by a country which repudiates obligations to banks, the IMF, or other lenders.[33]

The ATRR is triggered by classification of loans as value-impaired. As this category was defined, the major Latin American debtor countries were not subject to the value-impaired classification in late 1983 when the classifications were adopted (nor subsequently through November 1984). In contrast, the definitions contained in some of the earlier legislative proposals would have triggered a reserve requirement against loans to Mexico, Brazil, and Argentina.[34]

The ATRR and associated classification system does provide for consistent treatment from bank to bank; however, a very high level of distress is required to trigger the ATRR. This had the desirable effect in 1983 of avoiding a shock that would have occurred if international banks were required to write off 10 percent of their exposure to major Latin American debtors, and it also avoided disrupting ongoing restructuring arrangements. We do not believe that the agencies can be faulted for this, but it raises a serious question about the long run. The level of distress is pitched too high to have any significant ex ante constraining effect on country exposure.

But even if the definitions are revised, we believe a rigid classification system is inferior to a mark-to-market policy in encouraging prudent lending. A classification system exerts discipline on banks at discrete intervals after problems occur. A mark-to-market policy would operate continuously, disciplining both banks and borrowing countries and thereby reducing the probability that serious problems will occur.

33. Taken from Joint Press Release, Comptroller of the Currency, Federal Deposit Insurance Corporation, and Federal Reserve Board, "Interagency Statement on Examination Treatment of International Loans," December 15, 1983.
34. See, for example, H.R. 2957, The Export-Import Bank Amendments.

Amortizing Loan Fees

Perhaps the least controversial recommendation contained in the joint memorandum, incorporated in Title IX and subsequently implemented by the agencies, is that "front-end" fees on international loans be at least partially amortized over the life of the loans. Actual bank practice has varied widely on this matter and it has been argued that the practice of taking front-end fees on country loans into income in the year that they are paid has encouraged aggressive lending policies by banks because the performance of loan officers is often tied to current profits.[35] It is generally agreed that amortizing front-end fees in excess of front-end costs is good accounting practice.

Disclosing Concentrations of Country Exposure

In our view, the most important proposal included in the joint memorandum, mandated by Title IX and implemented by regulation, is to make information on country exposure concentrations publicly available. The country exposure report that the banks have been obliged to file semiannually since 1977 is now filed quarterly, and it includes a new section available to the public. The new section shows individual country exposures that exceed 1 percent of total assets or 20 percent of primary capital, whichever is less. The exposures are broken down by three categories of borrowers—public, banks, and other—and by period to maturity—less than and more than one year. In addition, when individual country exposures exceed 0.75 percent of assets or 15 percent of primary capital, the countries must be identified and the combined exposures reported.

Relating Required Capital to Country Exposure

The joint memorandum proposed that the federal regulatory agencies should "highlight certain large concentrations of credit" and factor these "into the evaluation of a bank's capital adequacy."[36] A bank with more exposure, in other words, would be expected to have more capital. Title IX requires that the regulators implement such an approach to evaluating capital adequacy.

35. Congress was also disturbed by the banks' charging "excessive" fees in connection with restructuring international loans. The final regulations distinguish between restructured loans and new syndicated loans, but the substance of the rule is the same for both types of loans.

36. Joint memorandum, Conover, Isaac, and Volcker, "Program for Supervision."

This is a superficially attractive proposal because it appears to be preventive in nature. Banks would be penalized when their exposures increased rather than when loans were in arrears as in the case of the ATRR. The joint memorandum, however, provided no hints regarding how this would be implemented. No regulations had been issued as of June 30, 1984, and reportedly the agencies were still struggling with the problem.

The difficulty comes at several levels. The first is that exposure cannot be factored into determination of capital adequacy in any demonstrable way except within the framework of a formal, quantitatively based system such as that used in Switzerland. There, required capital is calculated mechanically for each bank, based on the bank's composition of assets and liabilities. In such a system a capital increment based on country exposure could in principle be added to the total capital otherwise required. In a system in which required capital is judgmentally based it would be difficult to verify that taking account of exposure really matters.

In the United States the mix of mechanistic and judgmental components in the formulation of capital requirements has changed over the years. Since June 1983, the seventeen largest international banks have been subject to a minimum capital-to-asset requirement of 5 percent, but this has been scaled upward on a judgmentally determined basis. So long as this element of discretion remains, even if the agencies are conscientiously taking exposure into account, they may have difficulty demonstrating to Congress that they are doing so.

The second difficulty is in determining whether required capital should take account of the condition of borrowing countries. If required capital is based on exposure per se without regard to the existing condition of the country, the agencies will encounter the same problems that caused them to oppose country loan limits: "Such limits would fail to distinguish between countries capable of carrying substantial debt without significant transfer risk and countries where smaller amounts of debt still raise large transfer problems."[37]

On the other hand, if required capital is adjusted for exposure only to countries that have been classified as adversely affected by transfer risk, there is little reason to believe that ex ante decisionmaking by banks regarding exposure will be much affected. Overexposure is an ex post judgment; no bank intends to overexpose itself. Furthermore, raising capi-

37. Ibid., p. 9.

tal requirements only after a country has become reclassified has essentially the same effect as invoking the ATRR. Unless capital requirements are tied to exposure per se rather than to classified exposure, the proposed approach to capital evaluation will be redundant.

Increased Capital

Title IX also requires the following: "Each appropriate Federal banking agency shall cause banking institutions to achieve and maintain adequate capital by establishing minimum levels of capital for such banking institutions and by using such other methods as the appropriate Federal banking agency deems appropriate."[38]

Because the agencies had been wrestling with the capital adequacy problem for some years before the debt crisis and in 1983 took forceful measures to arrest the secular decline in capital ratios of major banks, it is not clear that the provision quoted above requires anything more. The problem for the agencies, as already noted, is to define capital requirements with sufficient precision that country exposure can be factored in and to develop a procedure for accomplishing this.

Assessment

In assessing the regulatory approach to the debt crisis we must distinguish different time horizons. In the very short term, the regulatory agencies succeeded in implementing legislative requirements in ways that did not have a significant effect on restructuring arrangements. The new regulations do not, of course, provide any mechanism for stimulating new money flows on a voluntary basis over the next several years. On the contrary, the incentive effect on new bank lending is bound to be negative, perhaps less so because of the specific restraints that were finally imposed than because of the atmosphere in which they were legislated. A much more punitive approach almost prevailed, and this political fact is likely to have a chilling influence as major banks plan how and where they grow in the years ahead.

But the most important issue is whether a useful framework has been put in place for preventing a repetition of the crisis. Here we are looking well into the future to a time when exposures will have been worked down

38. 12 U.S.C. 3907.

(or written off), and optimism will again have replaced pessimism in financial markets.

It is clear that the borrowing (demand) side of the equation is not affected at all. The need for an external control mechanism on country borrowing before the emergence of crises and the need for more flexible debt-financing instruments are not addressed.[39] The major thrust of the new regulatory approach is to constrain banks from becoming overexposed and to increase their ability to bear losses.

Under the new regulations, overexposure in the future would be constrained by public disclosure of heavy country exposure, by the prospect of required provisions to the ATRR, and perhaps by relating required capital to country exposure. The latter will not provide any additional constraint unless required capital is related to exposure per se as opposed to exposure to classified countries. These regulations will not have a direct effect on the behavior of borrowers. Our own proposals for secondary markets in country loans and mark-to-market policies would provide an additional ex ante deterrent to heavy exposures that would constrain both the borrowers and the banks.

Concluding Remarks

While the proposals for dealing with the debt crisis that we have developed may require modification in a number of ways, they do largely meet the essential criteria for effective policy actions. In contrast, the many other proposals that have received public attention are flawed in at least one of the following ways: they lack an effective means to keep money flowing to debtor countries as needed; they provide politically unacceptable subsidies before the need for subsidies is established; or they lack adequate structural reforms to prevent crisis situations from recurring. The task of developing a comprehensive program that meets the essential criteria should begin without delay. The current de facto policy of muddling through carries the risk that if existing arrangements break down, drastic actions may be required without adequate consideration of the long-run costs and benefits of various alternatives.

39. The need for better debt financing instruments is discussed in detail in Guttentag and Herring, "Commercial Bank Lending to Developing Countries."

Comments

William R. Cline: Jack Guttentag and Richard Herring have assembled in this paper an approach to the problem of international debt that seeks to bridge the gap between business as usual and radical reform. They reject, rightly in my view, many of the proposed schemes that would involve major writedowns and stretching out of developing country debt. They correctly note that these proposals would tend to choke off the flow of new capital to the borrowers.

However, Guttentag and Herring nonetheless recommend a program that could cause problems of its own. They advance a relatively radical plan because they consider the current lending system to be at great risk from an impending collapse of debt repayment by developing countries. The first question, then, is how likely such a collapse might be. Unless this likelihood is great, the disruptions caused by major changes of the type proposed could well cause greater damage than the actual risk would warrant.

In my view, developing country debt is manageable under the current strategy of temporary international lending to overcome illiquidity. Guttentag and Herring frequently mention "disaster myopia," the failure to see the impending collapse because none has occurred recently. But by 1984 the international economy was decisively in a phase of international economic recovery. That recovery should boost prices and quantities of exports from developing countries, enabling them to restore creditworthiness. Those who anticipate collapse would appear to be extrapolating into the indefinite future the trough conditions of the worst global recession since the 1930s. Such prognoses seem to suffer more from "recovery myopia" than the alternative estimates suffer from disaster myopia.

Consider the actual evidence from 1983. Mexico achieved a stunning turnaround from a current account deficit of $12 billion in 1981 to a surplus of $4 billion in 1983, far above the target of a $3 billion deficit. Venezuela achieved a current account surplus of $5 billion instead of the deficit of $3 billion or more that seemed likely initially. Brazil met its IMF target of a $6 billion trade balance surplus. The major debtors as a group

William Cline is a senior fellow at the Institute for International Economics, Washington, D.C.

performed well ahead of schedule, showing aggregate deficits less than half as large as had been anticipated. To be sure, much of this adjustment came at the expense of sharp reductions in imports associated with painful declines in GNP, and in the future it is essential that both exports and imports rise to permit reactivation of the economies. Nonetheless, progress to date is substantial, and domestic political tolerance to adjustment in debtor countries has held up surprisingly well. I suspect that historians will record November 1983 as the beginning of the trough of the debt crisis cycle; at that time the Brazilian congress accepted a compromise bill moderating wage indexation, thereby making it possible to reinstate lending by the IMF and other banks. In that case the debt problem was accurately handled as a liquidity problem. Yet implicitly Guttentag and Herring diagnose the problem as one of insolvency.

Correspondingly, the prospects for the banking system are showing improvement rather than deterioration. And although it is true that Guttentag and Herring's "quicksand effect" (which I call involuntary lending) does pressure the banks to keep lending, it is not true that they are throwing good money after bad or digging themselves in deeper. By providing modest new loans, banks can avoid default and shore up the old ones. Because their exposure is growing at a slower rate than the interest rate, the real present discounted value of their exposure is declining, not rising. These banks are floating up in the quicksand, not sinking deeper into it.

The particular reform package offered by the authors raises a number of questions. It is unclear to what extent the proposals are to be implemented on a voluntary as opposed to a mandatory basis. It seems unlikely that the program would overcome the most serious drawback of other radical reforms—the tendency to cut off new lending from banks. The more mandatory the program and the more remote it makes repayment schedules, the more unlikely it is that banks will be prepared to extend still more credit. Moreover, this program does not even accomplish the objective of reducing the real burden of the debt because, unlike other solutions suggested, it does not reduce the interest rate but instead delays indefinitely the amortization through replacement of existing loans by perpetuals. Yet amortization of principal is not a real burden because, under the rescheduling mechanisms now in place, old loans are being rescheduled or rolled over. While there is room for debate about the appropriate length of the leash (rescheduling two to three years of principal instead of just one, over ten years instead of eight, for example), there appears to be little case for making the leash infinite.

The marketability of the companion new assets—perpetuals issued with prior claim over old debt—would seem dubious. Market takers for Brazilian perpetuals at a limited interest rate spread above LIBOR (or even far higher spreads) would be rare, despite prior claim over past debt. Would buyers believe that their perpetuals would not be susceptible to similar subordination during the next round? Holders of past debt would of course strongly oppose subordination of their assets. Yet it is precisely these actors who are crucial to continued lending, especially if (as seems likely) the perpetuals for new debt achieved minimal market acceptance.

The motive for the perpetuals scheme is the authors' perception that the current mechanism of involuntary lending will not work in the future. Yet the robustness of that mechanism has been substantial to date. A full year after the initial breakdown in Brazilian debt servicing the banks were able to mobilize a $6.5 billion loan for Brazil with the participation of approximately 700 banks. Moreover, my calculations suggest that the major debtors should be able to return to voluntary lending by 1986–87.

If the involuntary lending does begin to suffer erosion from the problem of smaller banks acting as free riders (banks that perceive their individual action as not influencing the probability of the country's default, even though their combined action does so), the next appropriate step would probably be toward the capitalization of interest. Interest capitalization would automatically enforce full participation by all banks, who would participate by being informed of the fraction of interest capitalized instead of taking the direct action of extending new loans. This step should be avoided if possible because of its slide toward elimination of the remaining degree of voluntariness in the lending—at present, banks expect a country to present a coherent program before extending new loans. Nonetheless, interest capitalization would probably still be a viable basis for continued management of the debt problem, especially if conducted with some degree of IMF leadership and monitoring of country performance.

The recent strategy has appropriately treated each country individually. If a specific country encounters further difficulties, all parties return to the negotiating table to establish a modified program, involving more new lending by the banks and greater adjustment efforts by the country. The schemes that treat debt on a global basis, including the proposal by Guttentag and Herring, would tend unnecessarily to draw in countries that otherwise might be able to manage their debt under more traditional arrangements on an individually negotiated basis.

My last comment is that the authors' proposal to mark foreign assets to market seems likely to cause considerable destabilization. Markets for distressed external debt are thin, and extremely low values might be placed on these assets even though subsequently they could be honored, as the sharp recovery of Mexican external bonds since 1982 suggests. Appropriately, domestic assets experiencing sharp fluctuations from rising interest rates have not been subject to forced marking to market by the banks; it would seem unwise to enforce such requirements for foreign lending. Nor is the supposed tendency toward excessive foreign risk-taking a justification for asymmetric treatment between foreign and domestic assets: for some time to come, the problem will be that the banks are lending too little to developing countries, not too much, and the proposal of marking foreign loans to market would aggravate this problem.

Donald J. Mathieson: The paper by Guttentag and Herring contains both an interesting analysis of international bank lending and some useful reform proposals. There are two issues raised by their discussion, however, that in my view deserve further comment. First, the authors implicitly attribute much of the instability in international financial markets in 1981–82 to the fact that the profit-maximizing lending activities of international banks create an unstable adjustment process for the world economy. To minimize this potential instability, the authors propose a series of reforms that would, in part, place new restrictions on cross-border bank lending. There are alternative macroeconomic explanations of the recent instability that would suggest a quite different set of reforms. Second, the key element in the authors' reform proposals is the development of an active secondary market for perpetuals to be issued by debtor countries for both old and new debt. A basic question is whether this market would be viable without substantial official intervention.

Underlying the authors' structural reform proposals for the international banking system is the assumption that cross-border bank lending activities are inherently destabilizing and were an important cause of the disturbances in financial markets in 1981–82. It is argued that banks create this instability because they are unable to manage successfully the uncertainty associated with their international lending. These financial institutions thus tend to become vulnerable to large losses as a result of heavy concen-

Donald Mathieson is acting chief of the Financial Studies Division in the Research Department of the International Monetary Fund.

trations of risk exposure, weaknesses in the interbank markets, and the absence of effective controls on total indebtedness of borrowing countries. This hypothesis is discussed not only in the current paper but also in other papers by the authors and is similar to that developed by both Minsky and Kindleberger.[1] Many of the authors' reform proposals are designed to limit the scope of this potential instability by partially restricting the cross-border lending activities of banks.

One serious concern raised by this analysis is that the alternative explanations for the recent crises in international financial markets do not rest on the assumption that the international banking system is inherently unstable. This leads to a significantly different view of the types of reforms that are needed to avoid a repetition of the recent crises in financial markets. Moreover, there is little empirical information that allows one to determine which of these competing hypotheses provides a better explanation of recent events.

One major alternative explanation of the role of banks in the recent disturbances in international financial markets is that these institutions have been an efficient conduit for transmitting throughout the world economy the shocks generated by major commodity price changes, rising inflation and real interest rates, sharp shifts in monetary and fiscal policies in both developed and developing countries, and exchange rate instability. Cross-border lending was thus destabilizing only in the sense that the general macroeconomic shocks led to an adjustment process that made the servicing of international debts extremely difficult for many developing countries that are major debtors. Note that, if this alternative hypothesis is correct, the most appropriate reforms would be directed toward reducing the macroeconomic shocks to the system, especially those associated with poorly coordinated or inappropriate macroeconomic policies. While there would certainly be concern about increasing international bank lending, much greater attention would be directed toward the surveillance and coordination of policies across countries.

It is difficult to compare the relative importance of the hypothesis that

1. Jack Guttentag and Richard Herring, "Credit Rationing and Financial Disorder," *Journal of Finance*, vol. 39 (December 1984), pp. 1359-82; Guttentag and Herring, "Uncertainty and Insolvency Exposure by International Banks"; Hyman P. Minsky, "Financial Stability Revisited: The Economics of Disaster," in Board of Governors of the Federal Reserve System, *Reappraisal of the Federal Reserve Discount Mechanism*, vol. 3 (Washington, D.C.: Federal Reserve Board, 1972), pp. 95-136; and Charles P. Kindleberger, *Manias, Panics, and Crashes: A History of Financial Crisis* (Basic Books, 1978).

the banking system is inherently unstable and the hypothesis that financial instability emanates from macroeconomic shocks, because there is little empirical evidence concerning the determinants of the stability of the international adjustment process. In part, the absence of such empirical evidence reflects the difficulty of modeling adequately the international adjustment process as well as the lack of information on key variables such as the size and maturity of external debts. In the absence of empirical evidence, it seems surprising that the hypothesis of destabilizing bank behavior has gained such wide acceptance. Many of the banking system reforms proposed by the authors, as well as the policies of the legislative bodies of many major countries, appear to reflect the assumption of inappropriate bank behavior. Given our limited empirical knowledge, however, it would seem that some caution should be exercised in deciding which structural reforms of the international banking system are to be undertaken. If banks have primarily been a conduit for transmitting macroeconomic shocks, extensive structural reforms that seriously reduce the attractiveness of international lending to banks may contribute to an inadequate flow of resources to many developing countries in the remainder of the 1980s. This is not to argue that all reforms are bad. Even in the context of the hypothesis of macroeconomic shocks, there are good grounds for improved reporting and supervisory activities. What may be much less useful is actions that restrict or impose an implicit tax on foreign lending operations.

Perhaps the key element in the authors' reform proposals is the development of an active secondary market for perpetuals for both old and new debt of borrowing countries. Such a market is required for marking book asset values to current market values. A number of considerations suggest that increased official intervention would be required to maintain a viable market for these instruments. First, banks are not likely to accept readily the subordination of old or existing debt. Many of the oldest loans were made during periods when a given country's external position was strong and there was the prospect of sustained real output growth. If these earlier "correct" loans are subordinated along with all other "old" debt, this will create concerns that the perpetuals associated with "new" debts will eventually be subordinated as the country's government changes.

Another difficulty for the perpetuals market is the proposed linkage among the various necessary components: issuance of perpetuals, IMF lending programs, and the market prices of perpetuals. In the authors' proposals, the IMF would potentially be involved in the new system in a number of ways, including the purchase of a certain proportion of the new perpetuals as well as making sure that the new perpetuals are issued only when the country is following an IMF program. If such a system were established, the current market prices of the perpetuals would reflect to an important degree expectations regarding a country's ability to satisfy the IMF conditionality. Because the IMF programs are not always maintained and information about the status of the program becomes available only at discrete intervals, market prices may undergo sharp changes as expectations are revised. This type of price instability (or the possible suspension of market exchanges) would make it difficult to practice the concept of marking asset prices to market values. In most financial markets, price swings of this nature are minimized by the presence of speculators whose asset purchases or sales reflect a range of expectations about likely future asset prices. In the secondary market for perpetuals proposed by the authors, however, there would be sudden shifts in the available information set, and the views of all market participants regarding future developments are likely to change at the same time and in the same direction. The result is likely to be large price swings or the suspension of market transactions. These perpetuals could thus still represent assets embodying considerable country risk. Given the scale of the external liabilities of the major debtors among the developing countries, the level of official intervention needed to avoid these price fluctuations could be quite large, which would require a potentially large commitment of funds.

Nicholas Sargen: The paper by Guttentag and Herring presents a capsule statement of their views on the origins of the current problems in international lending, along with their suggestions for handling the situation and reforming the system. The authors have done a good job of identifying certain structural weaknesses in international lending and in providing a clear statement of the objectives to be met in tackling the current problem. They offer an innovative prescription for resolving the issue that is superior to most of the alternatives discussed. Nevertheless, for reasons to be discussed below, the authors' proposals for handling the immediate situation are not preferable to the current system of managed or coerced lending. Nor is it likely that banks will abandon the present scheme. The authors' suggestions for long-run reform of the system are more appeal-

Nicholas Sargen is vice president, International Bond Market Research Division, Salomon Brothers, Inc., New York.

ing. In fact, international finance already is evolving in some of the directions that they suggest. The main difference in approach that I would offer is the need to supplement greater oversight of international banks with increased surveillance over borrowing countries by the IMF and the World Bank.

In my remarks I focus on the three basic issues: factors contributing to the current problems, proposals for handling the immediate situation, and long-run reforms of international lending.

In their diagnosis of the current problems, Guttentag and Herring are primarily concerned with inherent structural weaknesses in international lending rather than with macroeconomic policies in industrial and developing countries that are at the heart of the matter. They identify several factors as sources of weakness, including heavy concentrations of credits, low spreads, transmissions of shocks through interbank markets, inability to control the overall indebtedness of borrowing countries, and uncertainties about lender-of-last-resort responsibilities. Their basic contentions are that banks suffer from disaster myopia, and that banks try to manage uncertainty by keeping their options open—lending to countries on short terms and keeping exposures and capital ratios in line with other international banks. The result, they argue, is that banks are vulnerable to adverse developments.

How accurate is this assessment of international lending? On balance, I share many of the authors' concerns, particularly about concentrations of bank credits to certain countries, low-risk premiums, "short-leash proclivities," and moral hazard problems in international lending. Their characterizations of bank behavior, however, are not developed sufficiently. In particular, a clear distinction should be drawn between two issues: how banks tried to cope with individual country risks, and how they tried to deal with systemic risks.

Banks as well as regulatory agencies and official institutions devoted considerable time and resources to identifying potential problem countries, with mixed results. However, they were far less successful in anticipating systemic risks that ultimately triggered the debt crisis of less developed countries. In particular, they did not anticipate that problems emanating from one or two countries would undermine market confidence and spill over to other countries. Banks, like many others, did not perceive the consequences of the shift in U.S. monetary policy in 1979 and sustained high real interest rates. They believed that they were protected from interest rate shocks because loans to developing countries were extended at variable interest rates. Instead, interest-rate risks, in effect, were transmitted back to banks in the form of country risks, as these developing countries were unable to earn sufficient foreign exchange to service their external debt.

From a policy perspective, the relevant question is whether anything could have been done to shield banks from these risks. The authors are correct that international lending problems were aggravated by increased concentrations of bank credits to certain countries. However, this was more a consequence of inherent difficulties in assessing sovereign lending risks than of disaster myopia in which lending risks are considered to be negligible.

The basic obstacle that banks encountered in making country-risk assessments was that the concept of debt-service capacity proved to be highly elusive. In the early 1970s, when lending to developing countries became more widespread, banks and official institutions typically analyzed various financial ratios—such as the debt-service ratio, reserve import cover, and the like—as part of a creditworthiness appraisal. These concepts were gradually downgraded, however, as developing countries acquired ready access to commercial finance. It was observed, for example, that countries with high debt-service ratios, like Brazil and Mexico, were able to service their debts while certain countries with much lower ratios, like Turkey and Zaire, encountered problems. Attempts to develop new ratios or guidelines through application of econometric techniques and other practices used in assessing domestic credit risks failed to develop reliable indicators and yardsticks to gauge country risks. The principal reason is that the incidence of debt reschedulings was too small to yield robust results. The outcome was that new standards did not take hold and creditworthiness appraisal increasingly became linked with judgments about access to private capital markets. "Herding instincts," in turn, were reinforced.

In light of the difficulties in assessing country risk, banks counted on portfolio diversification to reduce overall lending risks. Following the first oil shock, for example, loans to major oil-importing countries were balanced with credits to oil exporters. But portfolio diversification became increasingly difficult after the second oil shock, when lending to all developing countries far outstripped the growth of bank capital. Banks clearly bear some of the responsibility for permitting the increased concentrations of credits. However, responsibility must also be shared by policymakers and regulators in the industrial countries, who viewed recycling of funds through the international banking system favorably. This is especially true of the United States, where the stated objective of regulatory policy governing international lending was to avoid substantial concentrations of credits to countries.

What should be done to handle the present situation? The authors' prescriptions for resolving the problems in international lending separate short-run from long-run objectives. They reject the present scheme of managed or "coerced" lending as a way of handling the immediate situation because they feel it is bound to break down if regional or European banks refuse to participate in subsequent financing arrangements for problem countries. They favor a market-oriented approach to restore voluntary lending.

The proposals that Guttentag and Herring advance are preferable to many of the alternatives considered because they recognize the need to continue new flows of credits to developing countries in order to support adjustment efforts now under way. "The fundamental rationale for providing financial assistance during a stabilization program is that long-run elasticities are higher than short-run elasticities." The authors acknowledge that there may be solvency aspects to the problems of developing countries, but argue that, at least for the present, the presumption must be that the problems are mainly temporary. Their strategy is intended to buy time for developing countries to reduce debt-service burdens and for banks to lower concentration ratios and to amortize any loan losses. In this respect, the objectives they put forth are similar to the strategy currently being pursued.

The principal difference between the authors' proposals for handling the immediate situation and the present strategy is the manner (and speed) in which a market for voluntary lending is to be restored. A key aspect of the scheme developed by the authors is their willingness to subordinate existing claims to new claims. They feel this is necessary to provide incentives for new lending to the developing countries. However, there are several drawbacks with this approach.

One problem is that it is risky to establish a principle whereby prior claims are to be subordinated to existing claims. Such action is license for debtors to treat new, prior-claim certificates in the same way at some future time. Another problem is that for the authors' scheme (or most of the alternatives considered) to work, substantial amounts of new *nonbank* sources of finance to developing countries must be forthcoming. Otherwise, banks would merely be subordinating one type of claim on a country for another. (Loan contracts typically contain "negative pledge" clauses that prohibit preferential treatment among creditors for this same reason.) Yet it is difficult to identify new sources of such nonbank financing. Under present circumstances, in which debt-burdened developing countries are not deemed to be creditworthy, it is wishful thinking to presume that new creditors will step forth.

The main difficulty that I find with Guttentag and Herring's proposals for handling the immediate situation is that they are trying to restore voluntary lending prematurely. They suggest that banks could sell existing claims of developing countries; yet they acknowledge that any market for such claims is likely to be unduly depressed now. The risk of trying their approach now is that if some banks incurred sizable losses from selling existing claims, new bank lending to developing countries probably would dry up and additional sources of finances would not be forthcoming to make up the difference. The authors allude to the central role that the Federal Home Loan Mortgage Corporation played in developing an efficient secondary market for conventional home mortgages. It is also important to realize that the "securitization" of the residential mortgage market entailed: (1) the Federal Home Loan Mortgage Corporation guaranteeing participation certificates that savings and loan institutions exchange for mortgages; (2) regulatory changes allowing the savings and loan institutions insured by the Federal Savings and Loan Insurance Corporation to defer losses or gains from the sale of mortgages; and (3) "collateralization" of mortgage-backed securities. Hence, while the authors suggest that the IMF, the World Bank, or some new entity could play a similar conduit role in international lending, no institution has been willing to assume such a role because of the obligations it is likely to entail.

In short, a successful strategy for resolving the current crisis must be predicated on banks continuing to supply the vast majority of net new lending to developing countries until their creditworthiness has been restored. Indeed, the rationale for the current strategy of managed lending is that a precondition for restoration of voluntary lending is a significant improvement in the debt-service capacity of these countries. The strategy recognizes that considerable time is needed to restore voluntary lending, given the excessive indebtedness of many developing countries. In the meantime, the IMF will have to continue to play a central role by directing adjustment efforts in these countries and assuring that adequate new bank financing will be forthcoming.

This strategy obviously is not without risks. It presumes that conditions will improve over time such that the developing countries are better able to service their debts and banks can better absorb any losses. So far, at least, the strategy seems to be working. Certainly the debt situation today in these nations appears more manageable than when the crisis surfaced. U.S. interest rates are down sharply from their 1982 peaks, a broad-based U.S. recovery is under way, and commodity prices have begun to turn around. The external adjustment of developing countries has also far exceeded expectations, although trade surpluses in Latin America have mainly been attained through radical contraction of imports. Banks, for their part, have responded constructively by extending new credits to developing countries and rolling over existing obligations while also setting aside reserves and building capital. Dropouts and free riders have been kept to a minimum.

The principal risk is that, in view of the considerable time it will take some countries to restore market access, something could go awry. Thus even if developing countries continued to pursue their stabilization efforts, external factors such as oil-price or interest-rate shocks or political upheavals could further delay progress in restoring creditworthiness.

Banks are aware of this and have begun to develop a long-run strategy to handle the special problems of the most heavily indebted countries. There is growing recognition that debt reschedulings and provision of new money on a year-by-year basis may not be appropriate for countries that face large gross financing requirements in the future. Multiyear reschedulings and commitments of new money by banks could help reduce uncertainty and facilitate planning. Such programs and any interest rate relief, however, must be tied to IMF performance criteria to assure that structural adjustment is undertaken. The key to such an approach is tailoring programs to meet the specific needs of individual borrowers. More flexibility will be needed in financing packages to suit the particular needs of different types of commercial banks (such as regional and money center banks, European and U.S. banks) rather than treating all banks alike. The goal is to restore voluntary lending in stages. In the process, smaller banks that do not have long-term commitments to international lending will be able to reduce their exposures to developing countries gradually.

Many of the authors' prescriptions for long-run reforms of international lending are constructive and worthy of serious consideration. They call for the creation of a secondary market for bank claims, valuing bank loans at market rates, and increasing reliance on disclosure to help ward off a repetition of the current problems. The approach relies on improved information to discipline international lending.

Creation of a secondary market for bank loans is appealing, not only because of the information element, but also because it would make bank claims on countries more liquid and would "facilitate diversification of country loan exposures across institutions and individuals." Some of the problems encountered in assessing individual country risks could be reduced by an institution acquiring bank claims on countries and then issuing certificates against the entire pool of loans. This, however, would not protect the investor against systemic risks affecting groups of countries or poor assessment of individual country risks.

The international lending system already is being strengthened to some extent through the increased issuance of floating rate notes by sovereign borrowers and the development of a secondary market for these instruments. So far, the issuance of floating rate notes has been limited primarily to countries in relatively strong external payments positions (for instance, the Scandinavian countries and other smaller industrial countries) as well as to commercial banks. Few developing countries have been able to tap the market yet. Financial markets, in effect, have become segmented such that a voluntary, liquid market for creditworthy borrowers coexists with a managed, illiquid market for debt-burdened developing country borrowers. Recently LIBOR spreads in the market for floating rate notes have been driven down sharply as international investors search for scarce high-quality instruments.

As economic conditions in the developing countries improve, it is reasonable to expect that some of them will eventually be able to issue marketable floating rate notes. At that time, market valuation of their outstanding debt obligations—for market-related valuation that smoothed price fluctuations in the secondary market—could be considered. Valuing loans or notes of developing countries at market-related prices would not be subject to the problems discussed earlier in handling the special situation that currently prevails. In the meantime, however, any floating rate notes issued by debt-burdened countries most likely will be nonmarketable instruments.

A related issue that the authors consider is whether a market-oriented approach or recent regulatory proposals would be sufficient to prevent a repetition of the current problems. They are skeptical that the recent regulatory changes are adequate and are agnostic about the need to establish country lending limits to strengthen the regulatory framework. They thus ignore the strong case against setting formal country lending limits.

One problem is that limits are inherently arbitrary: there is simply no way of knowing ahead of time whether a limit is too restrictive or too permissive. A second basic problem is that lending limits would not allow the necessary flexibility to take account of differences in circumstances affecting borrowing countries or lending institutions. Moreover, it is most difficult to see how limits would be adjusted to take account of changing economic and financial market conditions that affect the ability of countries to service external debt or of banks to withstand financial shocks. In addition, there are obvious political ramifications from setting country limits, which are important for regulatory agencies to consider.

Rather than imposing arbitrary and cumbersome restrictions on banks or other financial institutions, the preferable route is to tackle the "moral hazard" problem in international lending directly by increasing the IMF and the World Bank leverage over borrowing countries. The expanded role would entail these institutions compiling more timely and comprehensive information on external debt, counseling countries on appropriate levels of external indebtedness, and improving their external debt management. To enhance this leverage, it is vital that the close working relationship between official institutions, the commercial banks, and central banks over the past year and a half continue to evolve *after* the IMF funds have been disbursed. In the event that countries do not follow the advice of the IMF or World Bank, these institutions must be prepared to make their views known to the financial community *before* problems develop. Once their views have been conveyed, either directly to commercial banks or indirectly through the various central banks and regulatory agencies, commercial banks must cooperate closely. In this way, new lending to debt-burdened countries and rollovers of existing obligations will continue to be tied to strict performance criteria.

In sum, there are essentially two ways in which problems of overlending or overborrowing can be avoided. One entails stricter control over lenders; the other, increased leverage over borrowers. Subsequent reforms are likely to entail both elements. However, the most practical and efficient route is to influence the decisions of individual borrowers rather than the collective actions of lenders.

Robert R. Bench and C. Stewart Goddin: As usual, Guttentag and Herring have produced another comprehensive and thought-provoking

Robert Bench is deputy comptroller for international relations and financial evaluations, and Stewart Goddin is senior international economic adviser, Economic and Policy Analysis Division, both at the Comptroller of the Currency, Washington, D.C.

paper. The authors should be commended on their efforts to develop novel financial instruments to alleviate the developing country debt burden. Nonetheless, most ideas in this vein, however appealing on the surface they may be, usually suffer a number of fatal deficiencies. Guttentag and Herring's prescriptions appear to fall into this category. The Guttentag-Herring paper also contains a somewhat unbalanced criticism of international as opposed to domestic bank lending (some examples of which are provided below).

The following brief observations and comments relate to three topics addressed in the Guttentag and Herring paper, namely, the structural weaknesses of international banking, the debt crisis, and the six-part proposal.[2]

Although excesses certainly do exist in international banking, the authors' views on structural weaknesses tend to exaggerate their importance. For example, some may believe that bank exposures to individual countries are high relative to capital, but these numbers pale when compared with those for industry or sectoral concentrations in domestic markets, which may also be subject to the contagion effect. Although there are uncertainties regarding lender-of-last-resort facilities and some parent banks are willing to assume responsibility for their foreign affiliates, the market has learned a great deal during the past years, resulting in more selectivity and caution in interbank placements.

The authors do, however, touch upon problems that have not yet been resolved: short-term lending, the herd instinct, disaster myopia, tardy entry by the IMF, and inadequate information. It should be noted, however, that the scarcity of information cited by the authors may be more of a problem for some regulators than for others. The United States receives exposure data on a consolidated basis and can obtain timely and accurate information about the overseas activities of U.S. banks through the U.S. examination process.

Our comments on the Guttentag-Herring evaluation of the debt crisis can be briefly stated. The "ad hoc" response to the crisis criticized by Guttentag and Herring, although perhaps unappealing in an academic sense, has basically worked. It has probably constituted the best response possible for dealing with the debt crisis during the past two years given institutional and time constraints. We agree fully with Guttentag and Herring, however, that progress is needed in finding more appropriate finan-

2. This version of comments by Bench and Goddin is based on an original version submitted in the form of an extended outline.

cial instruments and better institutional arrangements so that the past excesses can be avoided and the potential for future crisis reduced.

Guttentag and Herring's six-part proposal has a number of deficiencies and probably insurmountable hurdles. The initial ones have to do with their proposed new, marketable perpetuals certificates with prior claim. It is difficult to see how this proposal would actually work in practice. Beyond that, its purported advantages may well be outweighed by some obvious disadvantages.

The first of these disadvantages is that both banks and creditor governments would, we believe, be unalterably opposed to the concept of prior claim. Traditionally banks and governments have insisted on a policy of equal burden sharing in dealing with problem situations involving international debt. If the prior-claim concept were adopted, it would most likely lead to a severe contraction of "voluntary" lending by banks, governments, and suppliers—further exacerbating the debt crisis.

Although Guttentag and Herring assert there would be little risk that these new prior-claim certificates would themselves be subordinated in the future, the mere precedent established by these perpetuals would likely make the market skeptical of promises not to issue new perpetuals in the future. As a consequence, the marketability of the perpetuals would probably be affected, with the result being higher spreads to the developing countries and a worsening of the debt-service burdens of those countries.

The authors correctly point out that a critical element of their proposal is continued direct control and surveillance by the IMF until the perpetuals are retired. The IMF, however, has no enforcement powers besides moral suasion and its ability to withhold additional IMF funding. Except where countries needed additional financial assistance from the IMF, it is hard to see where discipline on individual countries would be forthcoming after perpetuals were issued. This, in turn, could raise severe regulatory and accounting concerns for banks that purchased these perpetuals. Banks would risk that their entire exposure in these perpetuals could subsequently be classified (requiring reserves or writedowns) should the country have a falling out with the IMF.

The authors also suggest that these perpetuals might well have a short life. If so, how do they really differ from the rescheduling arrangements now being concluded, which typically allow for four- to five-year grace periods?

Turning to Guttentag and Herring's proposal to transform old government debt into perpetuals certificates, we note two problems. First, the developing countries are unlikely to be willing to pay a penalty interest rate for the privilege of converting old debt into perpetuals certificates requiring continued IMF controls. Second, if these certificates have interest rate spreads at a higher level, rescheduled private credits will probably be penalized even more heavily, once again exacerbating the debt-service burden.

Adding further doubt to the acceptability of these perpetuals to the banking community is the suggestion that they be subject to an automatic writeoff policy. Such an automatic writeoff policy could very well tip the balance of leverage too far in favor of the developing countries. It could also provide them an excuse, if not an incentive, not to service these perpetuals promptly. Later, they could argue that they need not repay the entire amount of principal because it had been written off.

The authors make the argument that formulation of a general writedown system is immobilized under the existing system of coerced lending. This problem is even more acute in the case of the automatic writedown policy suggested for perpetuals. How would banks be expected to support new perpetuals sometime in the future if the old had in fact been written down?

The authors' proposed mark-to-market policy also raises several problems. First, there is virtually no secondary market for international loans. Marking to market therefore would mean marking to a volatile, thin market (see the authors' example in table 1). Second, consistency would require that domestic loans be marked to market, creating further challenges. Are the authors suggesting that banks appreciate the value of a particular loan on their books if the market price rose above par due to an improvement in creditworthiness?

The authors are correct in assuming that bank resistance to new lending would be stiffened if international lending were singled out for mark-to-market policy. We suspect their resolve might be sufficiently stiffened to get out of developing country lending altogether.

Finally, Guttentag and Herring's proposal to create a secondary market should be pursued further. The pooling mechanism that is suggested— whether or not organized by the IMF or the World Bank—might provide a means for tapping nonbank financial sources, but only if pricing, maturity, and legal problems could be resolved. We are not, however, in favor of absolute guarantees due to the discipline and "moral hazard" problems.

Authors' Afterword:
The Current Crisis
Reconsidered

AFTER completing a first draft of this paper in April 1983, we received comments and criticism from a number of persons, including colleagues from the Brookings Institution and the academic community, and from bankers and bank supervisors. The forums for such interchanges included conversations with individuals, informal seminars held at the Wharton School at the University of Pennsylvania, and a workshop on our research held at Brookings in January 1984. The authors of the comments included here all participated in the Brookings workshop. Our original plan was to revise our paper in response both to these extensive interchanges and to subsequent developments affecting banks, developing country borrowers, and the world economy. When Brookings decided to elicit and publish written comments on our paper, however, it seemed best to minimize revisions in the original version and to bring our views up to date in this postscript that takes account of issues raised by the commentators and others.

Sources of Instability

Several readers stated that we had unfairly blamed international banks for the debt crisis. This was not our intent. A balanced view of the causes of the crisis should surely apportion blame widely. Policy errors in borrowing countries help to explain why some countries have more serious difficulties than others, and policy errors in the major industrial countries along with the deterioration of the world economy help to explain why the crisis occurred when it did. Our focus is on the role of banks in the crisis rather than on an etiology of the crisis. We are concerned with why managers of major commercial banks permitted their institutions to become so vulnerable to cyclical fluctuations in the international economy and economic mismanagement on the part of a handful of borrowers, and

46

why the supervisory authorities permitted it to happen. Our objective is to suggest appropriate regulatory reforms.

Although we do not believe that international banks are primarily responsible for the crisis, neither do we agree with Mathieson that banks have been strictly passive conduits for transmitting macroeconomic shocks. The evidence that banks exercised a destabilizing influence is largely anecdotal and, admittedly, is not based on a comprehensive model of the adjustment process; nonetheless, it creates a presumption that bank behavior was not entirely passive. Perhaps the most striking evidence is the instances in which banks continued to lend in support of unsound economic policies long after residents of the borrowing country had demonstrably lost confidence in their government's policies. As a result, a large amount of bank lending was used to finance capital flight.

Furthermore, we believe we have put together some plausible hypotheses about *why* banks sometimes behave in a destabilizing way. These hypotheses are developed in greater detail in our previous studies. Many of the bank economists and lending officers with whom we have discussed these hypotheses have not only indicated general agreement, but have also provided us with supporting examples from their own experience. Sargen, in his comments on our paper, appears to agree with much of our analysis of structural weaknesses, except that he believes that excessive country concentrations were due less to disaster myopia than to "inherent difficulties in assessing sovereign lending risks" and, in particular, to the great difficulty of determining the risk linkages between countries. We have no quarrel with this point. In other work we emphasize mistakes due to inadequate information and analysis as strongly as disaster myopia.[1] In a world of perfect certainty, there would be no disaster myopia.

The Ad Hoc System and Prospects for Recovery

Our paper argues that the ad hoc arrangements that have been used to deal with the crisis are fragile and could collapse before the world economy recovers to the point at which confidence in the debt-service ability of

1. Jack M. Guttentag and Richard Herring, "The Insolvency of Financial Institutions: Assessment and Regulatory Disposition," in Paul Wachtel, ed., *Crisis in the Economic and Financial Structure* (Lexington Books, 1982), pp. 99–126; and Guttentag and Herring, "Commercial Bank Lending to Developing Countries: From Overlending to Underlending to Structural Reform," Brookings Discussion Papers in International Economics 16 (Brookings, June 1984).

the major borrowing countries is restored. As we perceived it at the time, the fragility arose from the tendency for smaller banks to defect from the arrangements in increasing numbers, leaving the most heavily exposed banks to assume an ever-increasing share of the burden. To some extent this has occurred. But because the amounts of new lending have been so small relative to the needs of major debtors, financial pressures have forced an increasingly painful contraction of aggregate demand, which has given rise to an even greater danger, namely, that economic and political pressures in the debtor countries will force a rupture in the already strained relations between the debtor country and foreign creditors. Although the consequences of such a rupture are uncertain, they may include diminished prospects for growth in many developing countries, a reduced volume of world trade, dislocations in export industries in many industrial countries, and the disruption of domestic banking systems and the international financial system.

William Cline has a much more sanguine view. He states, in his comments on our paper, "developing country debt is manageable under the current strategy of temporary international lending to overcome illiquidity . . . by 1984 the international economy was decisively into a phase of international economic recovery. That recovery should boost prices and quantities of exports from developing countries, enabling them to restore creditworthiness. Those who anticipate collapse would appear to be extrapolating into the indefinite future the trough conditions of the worst global recession since the 1930s."

We will not debate with Cline on the prospects for economic recovery of the debtor countries. We have little enthusiasm for a debate that we would prefer to lose. The issue, however, is not whether we are now past the economic trough, but whether future economic expansion will be rapid and strong enough to return the debtor countries to creditworthiness before the economic and political pressures in the debtor countries force a break in relationships with creditor institutions. In our view the potential costs of such an outcome are so high that it is important to develop a more flexible framework for managing the debt crisis until uncertainties in the world economy are resolved.

Cline is optimistic in his comments on the trend in bank exposure: "Because their exposure is growing at a slower rate than the interest rate, the real present discounted value of their exposure is declining, not rising. They are floating up in the quicksand, not sinking deeper into it."

Discussions with Cline reveal a significant conceptual disagreement between us on this point. Cline's argument is, essentially, that if a bank capitalizes interest, its true exposure does not increase because it has put up nothing more to lose. Thus if the country pays some interest net of new loan extensions, the bank's exposure must be reduced.[2]

Exposure measures the outstanding amount the bank has at risk. Although exposure can be measured in terms of either book value or market value, and one or the other may be more relevant for different purposes, Cline's argument is not correct on either measure.[3] Assume, for example, that a bank makes new loans in an amount less than the interest received on old loans, and that market value equals book value. Exposure increases on the basis of either market value or book value because both increase with the new loan. Alternatively, assume that market value initially is less than book value. Then exposure again increases based on book value, and it either increases or stays the same on a market value basis, depending on whether or not the market imputes any value to the increment in book value. There is no way, however, that exposure would *decline* based on market value.[4]

The end of the crisis depends both on improved economic prospects of debtor countries and, in the absence of institutional developments that will attract nonbank investors, on sufficiently reduced exposure by commercial banks that they become willing once again to become voluntary lenders. Even if the economic situation of the debtor countries improves substantially, banks have learned a stern lesson regarding risk linkages and consider themselves vastly overexposed at today's exposure levels.

Absolute measures of exposure are deficient in any case. Both banks and regulators tend to measure exposures relative to capital. Henry Terrell has constructed a set of simulations of U.S. bank exposure to non-OPEC developing countries as a percent of capital with projections to 1990.[5] Although exposure depends on a number of factors such as the financing requirements of these countries, growth of bank capital, and U.S. bank share of total financing, the simulations show that even under the most

2. The argument has nothing to do with inflation rates or relationships between outstanding indebtedness and bank capital.

3. In principle market value is preferable because it measures the amount that the bank's shareholders could lose if prospects for repayment worsen. Market values are often very difficult to determine, however, and many regulatory and managerial decisions are based on book values.

4. This does not imply that the bank should not make the loan. If a bank gets some cash flow from the debtor it is better off than if the debtor defaults.

5. Henry S. Terrell, "Some Considerations about the Future of International Lending" (Washington, D.C.: Board of Governors of the Federal Reserve System, April 1984).

favorable circumstances exposures of U.S. banks will decline slowly. For example, in Terrell's baseline case covering the nine largest U.S. banks, exposure declines from 230 percent of capital in December 1981 to 206 percent in December 1983 and to 193 percent in December 1990. These numbers provide no comfort.

The Proposal for Prior-Claim Perpetuals Certificates

Our proposal for developing perpetuals certificates with prior claim had the objective of stimulating an increased flow of credit to developing country borrowers in the short term. The prior-claim feature can be separated analytically and operationally from the perpetual feature. We focus on the former here because prior claim is the feature necessary to stimulate new lending. The perpetuals feature is discussed below with regard to new and outstanding country debt.

The prior-claim feature may entail significant costs, a point that our critics have emphasized. If one believes that costs will be high, then assumptions about prospects for recovery—whether one believes the optimistic scenario of Cline or a more pessimistic one—become an important consideration in assessing whether the prior-claim approach is worth the costs.

What are these costs? The main ones emphasized by our critics are associated with the possible precedent that would be established. First is the immediate impact on voluntary lending to countries still in good standing. In his comments Sargen notes: "Such action is license for debtors to treat new prior claims in the same way at some future time." How important is this? We are not sure. The existing restructuring arrangements have in many cases drastically altered repayment priorities from those contemplated by the market. Short-term trade credit and interbank deposits, in principle the most liquid and sacrosanct of all cross-border claims, have been treated in the same way as term loans in some reschedulings. Is there much difference between eliminating what was thought to be a prior claim and creating a new prior claim? We suspect that when the world returns to "normalcy," the market will view interbank deposits as highly liquid *except in a crisis,* and if prior-claim certificates are sold the market in the future will view other claims as subject to subordination in a crisis. That does not strike us as an undesirable outcome.

The fuzziness of the precedent cost should, in our view, be juxtaposed with the concrete and substantial costs now being borne by debtor countries attempting to improve their current accounts by curbing imports. The dangers that this poses to the political stability of these countries, to the sustainability of the conditionality principle, and ultimately to the world economy have been noted in many forums and require no elaboration from us.

Intimations from many quarters, including the Federal Reserve, that interest rates on debt of developing countries may have to be reduced in order to ease payment burdens indicate that this hazard is not being taken lightly. Our view is that if one accepts this premise, permitting subordination of their claims is much less costly to banks in the short term, and perhaps also in the long term, because such subordination means greater flexibility. On the assumption that the debtor countries will recover their creditworthiness in time, subordination will cost the banks nothing, whereas interest concessions are gone forever. Furthermore, interest forgiveness alone cannot provide debtor countries with any new money, whereas subordination would. On the assumption that these countries have the capacity at the margin to earn a foreign exchange return in excess of the market rate on new prior-claim debt, subordination increases the probability and rapidity of an eventual return to creditworthiness.

Restructuring Old Debt into Perpetuals

The proposal to convert old government debt and government-guaranteed debt into perpetuals that carry a penalty interest rate was designed to relieve liquidity pressures on debtor countries in the most flexible and least painful way possible. The proposal has been criticized on the grounds that the countries would not accept it because of the penalty rate or lenders would not go along because of their aversion to claims that never mature. In the meantime, however, sentiment has been growing to extend the maturities of restructured claims. For example, Irwin Kellner of Manufacturers Hanover Trust Company has stated, "The sooner we reduce the current ad-hoc reschedulings, the sooner confidence will return to both the banking system and the borrowing countries. That we are heading in such a favorable direction can be seen from the multi-year rescheduling of maturities now being negotiated."[6] Chairman Paul A. Volcker of the Fed-

6. Irwin L. Kellner, "New Fundamentals Have Bought Time," *New York Times,* June 3, 1984.

eral Reserve has lauded a "multiyear" agreement being negotiated with Mexico, referring to it as a possible "new phase" in the management of the debt crisis.[7] These comments raise an important question: if longer maturities on restructured debt are better, is the longest maturity not the very best? This question has caused us to rethink the issue of the optimum maturity on cross-border debt.

We define the optimum maturity as the maturity that minimizes default risk or, in other words, maximizes the probability that borrowers will meet their contractual obligations. Under the international arrangements prevailing before the crisis the optimum maturity reflected some balance between two conflicting pressures. If the maturity was too short the country was unduly exposed to short-run exogenous developments that affected its capacity to pay, or even market perceptions of its ultimate ability to pay. Preoccupation with meeting short-term debt repayment schedules, futhermore, would result in excessively short planning horizons and therefore in reduced productivity over the long run.

On the other hand, very long maturities would expose the lender to "moral hazard" by allowing the borrower the opportunity to undertake economic programs that jeopardize its future capacity to repay. The assumption is that borrowers are inhibited from taking such actions if they must renegotiate the loan after the creditor has observed their behavior and before they have reaped full advantage from their action.[8]

It is clear that in a noncrisis world the optimum maturity is not infinite so long as there is moral hazard.[9] In the absence of moral hazard, it would be infinite. If the country's growth rate exceeds the real interest rate on its debt, there is no economic reason for it to make net repayments of debt.

If debt financing were undertaken with marketable securities for which there were well-developed secondary markets (an integral part of our long-run restructuring proposal), the renegotiation discipline imposed by banks

7. Gordon Matthews, "Volcker Lauds Agreement on Mexican Debt," *American Banker,* June 7, 1984.
8. For further discussion see Guttentag and Herring, "What Happens When Countries Cannot Pay Back Their Bank Loans? The Renegotiation Process," *Journal of Comparative Business and Capital Market Law,* vol. 5 (June 1983), pp. 209–31.
9. We have also argued that actual maturities before the crisis were shorter than the optimum because of attempts by individual lenders to position themselves ahead of other lenders in the repayment queue, and that the divergence grew as a debtor country's economic prospects worsened. (Not until a crisis develops and restructuring agreements begin do lenders begin to act and think collectively, and even then bloc interests develop based mainly on differing degrees of exposure.)

could be replaced with market discipline as a means of controlling moral hazard. Under these conditions we believe the optimum maturity of such marketable debt would indeed be infinite.

When we shift our focus to a crisis state such as today's situation, the problem is quite different. Our original case for restructuring into perpetuals was that under crisis conditions the liquidity problem dominated the moral hazard problem, and if the crisis were resolved the penalty rate would suffice to prevent the moral hazard problem from reemerging in the future. In the current situation, however, restructuring into perpetuals would do nothing to relieve liquidity pressures because no repayments of principal are being made.

The main argument for restructuring with longer maturities during a crisis is that it reduces the number of required restructuring agreements. So long as de jure maturities remain short, frequent restructuring agreements are necessary, with the ever-present danger of an impasse that could lead to default. We concede, however, that it is not necessary to extend maturities to infinity to deal adequately with this problem, and our argument for restructuring old debt into marketable perpetuals is a long-run structural one requiring safeguards against the moral hazard problem that reemerges when the world economy returns to normalcy.

Valuation of Old Debt

In the paper we propose that the value of old (and subordinated) perpetuals be written down by 1 percent for every month that interest is delinquent. Bench and Goddin criticize this proposal because they believe debtor countries would be less willing to repay principal that had already been written off, and because they view it as unacceptable to banks.

The first point applies equally well to regulator-mandated writedowns such as the ATRR. The International Lending Supervision Act of 1983 and the regulations implementing it take no account of the effects of writedowns on borrower behavior. We believe that is as it should be.

Regarding the second point, the unacceptability of the proposal to banks, it seems likely that banks would prefer our proposal to the ATRR, both because our proposed policy is more certain and because banks would have more control. Banks can encourage a country to keep current by lending it some or all of the interest.

Mark-to-Market Policy

Our proposal to mark cross-border loans periodically to market has encountered two major objections from Cline and others. The first is that existing secondary markets are too thin to be reliable. We agree. As we noted in the paper, "A mark-to-market policy requires a market," and this proposed policy bears a symbiotic relationship to our proposal to create an efficient secondary market.

The second objection is the implied asymmetrical treatment of foreign loans as opposed to domestic loans. We believe such asymmetrical treatment is warranted by the special risks associated with foreign loans. It is a long-run proposal, however. Cline is quite correct in his comments when he states "for some time to come, the problem will be that the banks are lending too little to developing countries, not too much. . . ." The consequence of a period of overlending is always a subsequent period of underlending, the present predicament. Our proposal is not that mark-to-market accounting be adopted but that it be *developed* now for adoption when the period of underlending ends.

We are trying to avoid a common paradox of reform. Following a major shock, reforms become redundant because the previous excessive optimism has changed into excessive pessimism. Resources and attention are preoccupied with crisis management, that is, with minimizing the losses from the shock that has occurred. Over time as memories recede, losses are written off, old hands retire, and caution fades. As conditions reemerge for another round of excessive optimism, the perception of the need for reform also fades. Hence there is never a good time for this type of reform unless institutional momentum can be developed during the period of excessive caution.

Creating a Secondary Market

In general our proposal for creating a secondary market in country loans through a conduit agency has been received favorably. An exception is Mathieson, who foresees great difficulties in marking to market the perpetuals of countries subject to IMF conditionality because their markets would be thin and therefore secondary market prices would be subject to great volatility. This could well be true of old subordinated perpetuals, but in our scheme these would be subject to an administrative rather than a mark-to-market policy. In our view, the basic role of the conduit is to create efficient markets in loans of countries in good standing.[10]

As in the case of the mark-to-market policy, we regard the development of a conduit market as part of a long-term restructuring effort that would focus initially on loans of countries in good standing. Furthermore, we foresee great utility in the development of such a market, even in the absence of a mark-to-market policy, because the availability of published market quotations will have some constraining influence on banks as well as on countries. An effective secondary market will also encourage exposure diversification. And an effective conduit can use its market clout both to stabilize the demand for loans and to improve the types of loan instruments used in international lending. This last potential function of the conduit agency is developed in more detail in another recent paper.[11]

10. It is questionable whether the conduit should make a market in new, prior-claim perpetuals. In our scheme these instruments would be subject to the mark-to-market policy if they are acquired by banks, but we are not sure that a good secondary market will develop for such instruments.

11. Jack M. Guttentag and Richard J. Herring, "Commercial Bank Lending to Developing Countries."